A PROFESSOR'S GUIDE TO SUCCESS IN COLLEGE

A Professor's Guide to Success in College

Jeff Anstine, PhD

A Professor's Guide to Success in College

© 2017 by Jeff Anstine, PhD

The examples of people in this book are compilations of students the author has taught over the past twenty-five years. Any resemblance to any particular student is purely coincidental.

Windy City Publishers
2118 Plum Grove Road, #349
Rolling Meadows, IL 60008

www.windycitypublishers.com

Published in the United States of America

ISBN#:
978-1-941478-34-9

Library of Congress Control Number:
2016957982

WINDY CITY PUBLISHERS
CHICAGO

ACKNOWLEDGEMENTS

Thanks to Catherine Harris, Fernanda Valentino, Asley Lisak, Brian Lesiewicz, Matt Kozar and Matt Spicer for suggestions, Shelly Aschkenase and Ellen DeBerge for editorial help, and the helpful people at Windy City Publishers

CONTENTS

PREFACE

In over two decades as a college professor I have witnessed certain characteristics that separate students who succeed in college from those who do not. This book describes what students need to know and how to implement those actions to succeed in college. It is not about making college easy; college is not easy, a degree has to be earned. However, there are simple steps that can be taken to make the transition from high school to college smoother and the process of getting a bachelor's degree less complicated.

Internet sources and most college guides seem to have forgotten the basics of what college is about. Often their focus is on joining sororities, dealing with roommates or engaging in extracurricular activities. College is essentially about teaching and learning. This involves at least some, and sometimes a lot, of interaction between professors and students. At a bare minimum college success involves knowing a course's objectives and understanding a professor's grading expectations.

I provide a professor's perspective, on not just how to survive but how to excel in college. The latter chapters provide guidelines for what to expect in classroom situations, how to choose classes and recommendations for studying for tests and writing papers. In addition, I supply tips on how to get the most out of both your classes and the college experience.

chapter 1

INTRODUCTION

Acollege[1] degree has never been more important. High school students and their parents realize this: thus there were over 20 million students attending American colleges and universities in the fall 2015.[2] On average, workers with a college degree earn almost twice as much as those with only a high school degree. Thus, over a lifetime college graduates earn over a million dollars more compared to those without one.[3]

Obviously there is more to life than money. Research also shows that people with college degrees enjoy life more. They tend to have a higher level of self worth and confidence. They are more curious and more open to new experiences. College helps individuals develop a better sense of who they are and where they fit in the world.[4]

Though students and their parents recognize the importance of a college degree, many students still fail to reach this goal. As many as one-third of college First-year students do not return for their second year.[5] Only half of the students who start college graduate. In some cases it is because students forget what college is about or do not know in the first place. Sometimes there is a tendency to make things too complex, losing focus of what matters. Ultimately, succeeding in college depends on being able to learn from the people responsible for your education, the professors.

---

1 Throughout this book I will mostly use the word college to describe institutions of higher education. You will see later that a college is different from a university. I just use college to simplify it.
2 National Center for Education Statistics
3 *New York Times* May 27, 2014
4 College is certainly NOT a requirement for people finding their identity, enjoying their life, and having a successful career. This book in no way is intended to denigrate occupations that do not require a college degree. I have nothing but respect for anyone who puts in a hard day of work at any job.
5 *US News and World Report* http://colleges.usnews.rankingsandreviews.com/best-colleges/rankings/national-universities/freshmen-least-most-likely-return

In new situations it often takes a while to adjust, adapt, learn and finally to excel in our endeavors. I provide guidance for what to expect in college so that the process is easier and more rewarding.

Many people who are successful in life tend to be proactive. They have the ability to navigate jobs and careers because they know what to expect. They are able to look ahead and prepare. Less successful individuals are reactive; a problem arrives, then they try to solve it.

I have seen many college students struggle because they are reactive. They spend a lot of time and energy responding to a situation that they should have been ready for. They fail a class because they don't understand what the professor wants, or they need to take another year to finish college because they were not aware of graduation requirements. Some flunk out because they do not know how much time they need to spend studying for classes or where to focus their energy in a particular course.

College is a great place to learn how to navigate life. There is usually a low cost associated with a mistake, a low grade on a test (that I will explain how to correct) or a reprimand from a Resident Assistant. Receiving an F in a class or being dismissed from school typically has a high cost. There is often an upside from a negative experience, if you are willing to learn from it.

> COLLEGE IS A GREAT PLACE TO LEARN HOW TO NAVIGATE LIFE. PERHAPS MOST IMPORTANTLY, COLLEGE IS A TIME TO LEARN ABOUT YOURSELF.

If you take control of your college experience, you get a lot out of it. As with life, there are some things you can control and other things you can't. I will explain these throughout the book. College is a time to learn skills for future jobs. It is also a time to learn how to communicate, think critically and discover the world. Perhaps most importantly, college is a time to learn about yourself.

There are hundreds of books and websites on how to get in to college, what types of extracurricular activities college admissions officers are looking for, how to increase college entrance test scores, and on writing the essay that will get you into the right college. There is also information on roommates, sex in college, and how to join fraternities and sororities. There are also many sources about saving and paying for college. You get the idea. However, there are very few books about how to succeed once you are in college; and almost no books written by full professors for students. This is surprising given the fact that only half of the students who start college actually earn a degree.

For many students, college is the first time they experience failure. Many students (and their parents) think that because they made it through high school, they will make it through college. Average, good, and even very good students fall into this trap. Some students think college classes will be similar to high school classes and do not adjust to the differences. Other students have difficulty following lectures. Still other students don't even know they need help in a class or are not sure what to do if they are doing poorly. Professors are amazed by the number of students who receive an F in their class at the end of a semester, not realizing that they were failing it all along.

I often hear the parents of incoming first-year students say things like, "He did great in high school, I am sure he will do the same in college." "She's the creative type, her talents were stifled by high school teachers, but college professors will encourage her creative side." "He struggled a little in high school, but he's much more mature now, so he'll do fine." "I made it through college with no problems, so I am sure my kid(s) will too." "We've provided so much support (monetarily and emotionally) that I am sure s/he will finish."

Students will say, "I took advanced classes in high school, I'm sure the classes in college aren't any harder." "I didn't do as well as my parents expected in high school, but it was because the classes were too constricting, I'll do fine in college where I have more options."

Less than two percent of first-year students believe that they will drop out of college temporarily or permanently.[6] Yet, hundreds of thousands of students flunk out their first year. Others struggle on academic probation for a year or two before dropping out. Some students drop classes each term or switch from full-time status to part time, spending lots of money over a period of four or five years and still do not finish. And still other students take six or more years to finish, piling up significant debt along the way.

There are lots of reasons why perfectly capable, bright students do not finish college. Many students make the mistake of thinking that since they made it

---

6 American Council on Education "The American First Year Students: National Norms"

through high school, they will make it through college, so they do not take college work seriously. Other students flunk out or do not do well because they do not know how to "do" college; they don't learn how to navigate the system.

For others, the non-academic adjustment from high school to college is much more difficult than they expect. Some encounter unforeseen problems and do not know where to go for help. It is not that these students are not smart enough, it just that they are not prepared for the academic and non-academic challenges they face. I will provide solutions to all of these problems later in the book.

In grade school and high school there is a fear of holding students back; so the tendency is to pass students even if their work is unacceptable. Many college professors have no problem flunking a large number of their students. A college degree needs to be earned and professors will not pass those who do not meet their standards.

Many students are shocked to find out that if they do not do the required work they will fail a class. There are always excuses from these students. "The tests in that class weren't fair." "That teacher was just out to get me." "I didn't understand what the professor wanted."

As a professor who has taught thousands of students, I believe that practically every student who starts college can finish. The key is taking responsibility for individual success. In a college class, two people are responsible for a student's education—the professor and the student. You have little, if any control over what the teacher does. However, you have complete control over what you do. This book will provide advice for how you as a college student can take control of your college career.

chapter 2
COLLEGE, SUCCESS, AND LIFE

W hat is important in your life? For many of us part of the answer certainly entails making a decent salary and having a well respected job. Colleges are the gatekeepers of future success in this regard since it is impossible to be a high school teacher or a lawyer without a college degree. But what we value goes beyond simply money and a career. For most of us family, friends, religion, and other factors also play a major role in satisfaction with our lives.

Maintaining an attitude of gratitude and knowing how to enjoy what the world has to offer is also essential. College experiences, in and out of the classroom, help us appreciate all there is to life. One of the best aspects of the college years is the opportunity to learn about yourself, the world, and where you fit in it.

The college experience encompasses a multitude of matters. Knowledge acquired goes far beyond obtaining skills for a job. The ultimate goal is personal happiness with who you are and what you do with your life. You don't need a college degree to be happy. But college opens doors that might otherwise remain shut to you. The knowledge, skills, and options a college degree provides gives you greater control over your life. Successful individuals direct their own lives and tend to be more content than those who feel stuck with where they are unable to make meaningful changes in their lives.

> THE KNOWLEDGE, SKILLS, AND OPTIONS A COLLEGE DEGREE PROVIDES GIVES YOU GREATER CONTROL OVER YOUR LIFE.

How do you define success? For some of us it is based on the number of friends we have or the amount of time we spend with our kids. Success can be measured by personal growth and satisfaction. Career success depends on of a variety of factors, some of which we can control and others which we do not. Some people are born with special talents that enable their accomplishments as musicians or artists. Others are born with skills that allow them to hit a baseball thrown a hundred miles an hour. Even these lucky individuals need to practice, however, to excel in their fields.

For the majority of us, our success will depend on intelligence and hard work. But even these factors are not always enough. Some smart, enterprising individuals struggle to get ahead in life because their efforts are misdirected or they are unable to manage frustrating situations. Others find their goals jeopardized because they do not work well with other people, they lack perseverance or they give up when facing obstacles.

There are many skills you gain in college that are necessary for your future success throughout your life. At the very minimum you learn how to: think critically, communicate well and write effectively. College is also a great place to practice perseverance, learn where to focus your efforts and how to work with others. It can also help you develop your own unique perspective on the world.

Regardless of your career choices, circumstances, these skills will serve you well. Perhaps even more importantly you will learn how to learn. In this rapidly changing world, you will need to know how to keep up with new ideas, how to process them and how to use them.

Long before you start college and up through graduation you will be pressured by many people. Parents, siblings, friends, a boyfriend or girlfriend, teachers, guidance counselors and others will tell you what they think you should do. They will tell you which school you should attend, which classes you should take, what major you should declare and maybe even what you should do with your life. **You should listen to people who offer you advice, then decide for yourself what to do.** Your success in college and beyond depends on decisions you make that are best for you.

There are two parts to success in college: doing well in the classroom and adjusting to life as an independent young adult. **There are two basic things you need to master in order to succeed in college academically. The first is to develop beneficial habits such as effective time management.** If you practice managing tasks expeditiously while in school, later in life your ability to complete projects in a timely manner will lead to career and life success. You need to understand how to budget your time, and use it wisely.

THE SECOND KEY TO SUCCESS IS UNDERSTANDING YOUR PROFESSOR'S EXPECTATIONS. This entails listening carefully to your professors, knowing the course requirements and ensuring you carry out all the required tasks (tests, papers, presentations, etc.). There is often miscommunication between children and their parents, friends, and in many other interactions. Don't let a simple misunderstanding cost you a good grade. If you do not understand something, ask.

Matters learned outside the college classroom are often just as important as those learned within. In fact, you will spend more time out of the classroom than in it and more time engaging in non-academic activities than in academic work. During your college years you will experience significant self-discovery. College is a great time to develop your identity, to figure out why you are special, and to appreciate what makes you unique.

REMEMBER...

LISTEN TO PEOPLE WHO OFFER YOU ADVICE;
THEN DECIDE FOR YOURSELF WHAT TO DO.

DEVELOP BENEFICIAL HABITS,
SUCH AS EFFECTIVE TIME MANAGEMENT.

UNDERSTAND YOUR PROFESSOR'S EXPECTATIONS.

chapter 3
TYPES of COLLEGES and UNIVERSITIES

Selecting the right institution is critical to success for many students. While this sounds obvious, some people don't know there are significant differences between colleges. Even if you have already chosen a school, this section will provide a useful overview of what to expect. If you are still undecided, this chapter will help you narrow your choices.

Just like there are many types of companies (large corporations, non-profit organizations, etc.) there are a variety of higher educational institutions. Just as individuals will thrive in a particular work setting, there are certain colleges or universities that fit some students better than others. WalMart, Apple, and Ford are great work environments for many people. Others, however, function better at other firms. Stanford, the University of Michigan and other well-known schools will be the best fit for some students, yet there are hundreds of lesser known schools that will be a better fit for other students.

One reason some students don't succeed is they are in the wrong place. High school students face pressure from family, friends, guidance counselors, and others to choose certain schools because of proximity, family ties, finances, or other reasons not necessarily related to what the student wants or needs.

PICK THE RIGHT SCHOOL FOR YOU

A student who went through the process said, "I should not have been so anxious about who picked me: I should have been anxious about whom I picked."[7] Some students get so wrapped up in what school they think they should attend that they don't pick one that is the best for them. If you have

7 Chronicle of Higher Education Feb 25, 2005, p B35

not chosen a school yet, select carefully. If you are already attending college and are absolutely certain that this is not the place for you, transfer to one that is a better fit.

IF YOU ARE ATTENDING A SMALL COLLEGE, ENGAGE IN ACTIVITIES THAT MAKE IT SEEM LARGER. Join clubs, get involved in extracurricular activities and study abroad. You will meet different people and do things that will broaden your college experience. **IF YOU ARE AT A LARGE UNIVERSITY, MAKE IT SMALLER.** Ironically, the same advice holds, join groups and get involved. This way you will meet students with similar interests, making the university less daunting.

TYPES OF POST-SECONDARY INSTITUTIONS

The Integrated Post-Secondary Education Data System (IPEDS) defines a post-secondary institution as an organization that is open to the public and has as its primary mission the provision of post-secondary education or training beyond the high school level.[8] Colleges and universities provide post-secondary education and while often used interchangeably are different. Officially a college is an educational establishment for higher or professional education. A college is also an independent part of a university. A university is an educational institution, composed of one or more colleges and graduate schools that provides instruction and facilities for research in many branches of advanced learning and awards degrees.[9]

To make it even more confusing, in some cases a school is called a college but is more like a university. This information follows the Carnegie Classification because it is the system that colleges and the National Center for Education Statistics (NCES), the primary federal entity for collecting and reporting data related to education, in the United States, use. This system is also used by *U.S. News & World Report* and other sources that provide information about higher education.[10] Though each school is unique, there are broad categories into which they are categorized.

---

8 http://nces.ed.gov/ipeds
9 *Oxford American Dictionary*
10 "To rank colleges and universities, *U.S. News* first assigns schools to a group of their peers, based on categories developed by the Carnegie Foundation for the Advancement of Teaching." *US News* website. For example the *U.S. News* calls the Doctorate-granting institutions National Universities.

Contrary to popular belief for all universities and many colleges, teaching undergraduates is not their only purpose. In some cases, particularly at national universities, it is not even their primary purpose. Public universities were set up to promote the arts, to help solve problems in the community, to perform research and to work on areas that improve the public's understanding of current issues.

There is a difference in the culture at each school. There is also a difference in the number of degrees offered, support for students and other factors influencing student satisfaction and success. In addition to its website, one way to find out about each institution is to look at the mission of the college and use higher education guidebooks.

Generally large universities focus on research and smaller colleges emphasize undergraduate education. However, this has changed significantly over the past decade. Now, national universities have worked hard to improve undergraduate education, and Liberal Arts schools' faculty are conducting more research.

National Universities

Most post-secondary school information focuses on the large state universities, such as the University of Illinois, or large, well-known private schools like Yale. These schools typically offer a large number of undergraduate degrees. Their large size also affords opportunities to enjoy numerous extra-curricular activities and events.

Research, obtaining grants, and other non-teaching activities serve as primary job responsibilities for professors at these universities. Professors at these institutions engage in pursuing knowledge in order to better understand and explain the world. They are rewarded almost exclusively for publications and the grant money they bring into the school. Many of the professors do not teach introductory classes, and if they do they are large classes of 100, 200, or more students in a lecture hall, with graduate students grading the material.

There are many great reasons to attend a National University, but keep in mind that typical undergraduates at these schools do not get much attention from professors. Thus at a large university, students taking introductory classes receive the least amount of contact with full-time tenured professors. Teaching Assistants, typically graduate students, teach a large portion of these introductory classes.

Regional Universities

While national universities get much of the publicity based on their size, prestige, sports programs and sometimes affiliation with a state, the majority of students attending college go to regional universities, small private schools and community colleges that are typically only known locally. One of the best aspects for an undergraduate attending a regional university or smaller college is that these schools focus more on teaching. Here, students have more interaction with professors, sometimes even informally outside traditional avenues.

If these schools offer advanced degrees, they are usually Masters Degrees, though some grant a limited number of Doctorates. These schools typically have a large number of course offerings for undergraduates, but still not as many as at research universities. Since these institutions focus more on undergraduates, they typically have more full-time professors in introductory classes. Another benefit is that class sizes are usually limited to forty-five or thirty-five students.

Liberal Arts Colleges

To be classified as a Liberal Arts College, at least half of the degrees granted have to be in English, literature, languages, economics, math, biology, and other areas in the humanities, social sciences, and natural sciences. Usually undergraduate students get more guidance with selecting classes, writing papers, and other academic endeavors. Usually with more interaction between students and faculty, there is a strong sense of community at these schools.

Regional Colleges

Regional Colleges also offer degrees in the Liberal Arts, but over half of the degrees granted are in areas other than the humanities, social sciences, and natural sciences such as in accounting or education. There is more interaction with professors and more of a community feel that helps support student development.

Associate's Colleges/Community Colleges/Junior Colleges

While almost half of all students attend Associate's Colleges, these are the least understood. Four-year non-profit colleges provide students with a broad education and preparation for specific careers. Many Associate's Colleges and the majority of for-profit schools provide technical training. Technical training teaches students how to perform certain tasks, such as how to be a dental assistant or lab technician, that lead directly to a job. Some classes can be transferred to a four-year school toward Baccalaureate Degrees. Some students opt to spend a year or two at these schools to save money before transferring to another institution.

FACULTY EDUCATION AND LEVEL OF COMMITMENT VARIES AT ALL TYPES OF SCHOOLS BUT THERE IS MORE VARIATION AT ASSOCIATE'S COLLEGES. Some professors have PhD's but most don't, though the majority do have Master's Degrees. The majority of faculty are committed to their students but increasingly many are hired on a temporary assignment. These faculty are the least appreciated in higher education. In addition, there is an enormous amount of variation in the student body that can present particular challenges. The ages of students may range from seventeen to seventy, many students are first in generation to go to college and many have family and work obligations.

It is important everywhere, but particularly at **ASSOCIATES COLLEGES TO MAKE SURE YOU KNOW WHAT YOU WANT OUT OF YOUR CLASSES.** If you are preparing for a certificate program make sure all of your classes count towards this and that you manage the schedule for any required certification exams.

IF YOU ARE GOING TO TRANSFER TO A FOUR-YEAR COLLEGE, MAKE SURE THE CLASSES YOU TAKE COUNT AT AN ACCREDITED UNIVERSITY OR BACCALAUREATE COLLEGE. The numbering system that colleges use varies from school to school, but the college should have a list of which classes transfer. Make sure you find the articulation agreements between your two-year school and the four-year one. This information is available on the schools' web-sites and in the Registrar's Office.

OTHER SPECIALIZED POST-SECONDARY INSTITUTIONS

In addition to the types of colleges I've just discussed there are hundreds of specialized institutions that include theological seminaries, schools of art, music, and design, medical schools, and tribal colleges and universities. These organizations grant degrees from Associate's to Doctorates, but are typically in a single, specialized area.

Private and Public

THE MAJORITY OF COLLEGES ARE NON-PROFIT, WHICH MEANS THAT THEY USE ALL OF THEIR RESOURCES FOR PROVIDING THEIR SERVICE AND ARE NOT OUT TO MAKE MONEY FOR OWNERS, SHAREHOLDERS, OR OTHERS WITH A STAKE IN THEIR ORGANIZATION. Public institutions get part of their operating budgets from the state in which they are located; thus they are beholden to some degree to state officials on how they spend their money. Private schools also get some money from public sources, but do not receive money directly from the state in which they are located. As a general rule, private schools are more expensive than their public counterparts.

The percentage of their budget that public colleges receive from state funds has dropped significantly over the past few years. The result, not surprisingly, has been large, sometimes double-digit percentage, increases in tuition. So while private colleges are also increasing tuition, the price differential is not as great as it was. In addition, on average private schools give more aid so the tuition actually paid is closer to public schools than what is listed.

THE LISTED TUITION IS NOT NECESSARILY WHAT YOU HAVE TO PAY. IN SOME CASES YOU CAN NEGOTIATE, especially if you are a good student or unique in some way (play a certain instrument, etc.). There should be a net cost calculator on the school's website that will provide a general idea of your cost of attendance. Be sure to find the net price for the schools you are considering. Also be aware that there can be large differences in the discounts that students get at a particular school.

For-Profit Universities

DeVry Inc. and the University of Phoenix are among many for-profit universities. **UNIVERSITIES RUN FOR-PROFIT MEANS THAT IN ADDITION TO PROVIDING EDUCATIONAL SERVICES, THEY ARE ALSO OUT TO MAKE MONEY FOR SHAREHOLDERS—JUST AS APPLE AND MICROSOFT DO.**

For-profit universities may have their place in higher education, particularly for working adults. Be aware of the differences between these and traditional schools. On the positive side, they offer flexibility and support for adult learners. A large negative is that the University of Phoenix recruiters are paid based on the number of students they sign up. Another difference between for-profit universities and traditional schools is that they don't have other non-academic opportunities, such as clubs, sports teams, and other extracurricular events.

In the spam buried between the emails about the next hot stock, improved sexual energy, and magic potions that will melt away pounds, you will invariably find ones guaranteeing you your college degree. There are scams everywhere, and if there is an opportunity to make a quick buck you can be sure somebody is taking advantage of it. Considering how easy it is to make fake Gucci bags and Rolex watches, and how easy it is to fake a degree, it is surprising that there aren't more knock-off or fake degree solicitations swirling through the multi-million dollar diploma mill industry.

By completing a questionnaire, describing your life experience, and sending a few thousand dollars (or more), you can receive a degree from Saint Regis or Columbia State University. Sound great? Saint Regis University is based in Liberia, and operated by shady characters from within the US. These schools are not recognized by accreditation agencies, and the diplomas they're selling are worthless. If you decide to attend a for-profit university, watch out for diploma mills. In addition, **BE AWARE THAT A NUMBER OF THESE SCHOOLS ARE AT RISK OF LOSING THEIR ACCREDITATION.** They will lose government funding, and classes taken there will not transfer to other colleges. **BE SURE THAT ANY SCHOOL FOR WHICH YOU REGISTER WILL REMAIN ACCREDITED.**

RANKINGS

College rankings can be useful but **BE WARY OF HOW SCHOOLS USE RANK-INGS.** Schools will include or omit variables in order to improve their image. Remember, schools are trying to woo you. This is not to say that you should not go to Harvard if you get in (I know I would have). **THERE IS MUCH MORE TO A COLLEGE THAN WHAT YOU SEE IN THE VARIOUS RANKINGS.** The rankings tend to be based on variables that do not measure learning in college, such as SAT and ACT scores and high school GPA. For example, *Business Week, The Wall Street Journal and the U.S. News & World Report* all rank Business Schools. Each uses a different system. Each uses different variables that they think are important and each is weighted differently.

Rankings have remained fairly consistent over the past twenty years. Unfortunately one of the unintended consequences of the system is the devaluation of education provided by schools not at the top of the rankings. You can get a great education and grow as a person at practically every college in the country.

DO NOT WORRY IF YOU ARE NOT ATTENDING AN "ELITE" OR "BRAND-NAME" SCHOOL. Alan Krueger at Princeton University says, "What students should not do is assume that the right college for them is necessarily the one with the most prestigious name." The *Boston Globe* also offers salient advice: "…because so many students attend graduate or professional school after college, the choice of an undergraduate institution is less significant than it used to be."[11] Believe it or not, Steven Spielberg was rejected by his first college choices—USC and UCLA. He attended Cal State Long Beach, which certainly has not diminished his accomplishments.

GRADES

Generally grades have risen at all colleges and in most departments over the past few decades. This grade inflation receives regular media attention and has even been lampooned by "Doonesbury" comics. Some schools hesitate to give Ds or Fs. Even within universities, some colleges or departments are more likely to

---

11 March 17, 2002

give As and Bs—or refuse to give Ds and Fs—than other departments within the same college. Professors are rewarded (at least in part) by how students rate them. If professors give better grades, then the students will like them more and give higher evaluations of the professors.

Even with grade inflation, about half of all students do not graduate. I believe that one of the major reasons is that many students attend a college that is not a good match for them. It is critical to find the right fit for you (just as it is with a spouse or a job). **If you are not succeeding at your present school, find one that suits your needs.** The school's culture plays a major role in students' success. If you are struggling or are unhappy where you are, consider transferring. Make sure you spend enough time picking the school that will be the best fit.

REMEMBER...

IF YOU ARE ATTENDING A SMALL COLLEGE,
ENGAGE IN ACTIVITIES THAT MAKE IT SEEM LARGER.

IF YOU ARE AT A LARGE UNIVERSITY,
MAKE IT SMALLER.

BEYOND YOUR DEGREE, WHAT ELSE DO YOU WANT
OUT OF COLLEGE?

chapter 4
HOW TO PREPARE FOR COLLEGE

There are few similarities between high school and college. This isn't to say that high school doesn't prepare you for college, it is just different. Learn as much as you can about the college you will attend before you start classes. If you know someone who has gone to this school, talk to them.

College administrators know that providing accurate, current information and helping students transition from high school is integral to students' success. So, there has been an increased emphasis on web-based assistance over the past decade, including information on financial aid, classes, student activities, events, and other essential topics. Spending time familiarizing yourself with the website is highly beneficial. **USE THIS RESOURCE.**

Handy as the internet may be, other key information sources can be experienced only in person. **SPEND AS MUCH TIME ON CAMPUS AS YOU CAN.** If possible, make an overnight visit. Attend a class in a subject area that interests you. Talk to current students. Visit the student center, eat at the cafeteria and wander around the library.

Every college offers orientation programs to prepare incoming students for college. These sessions are typically held over the summer, usually the week before the semester's classes begin. At a minimum, schools will provide seminars teaching new students the basics on how to register for classes, where to park, how to use the food service, etc. Increasingly, the orientation programs last days or even a week. **GO TO ALL OF THE ORIENTATION SESSIONS**, even the ones that are not mandatory. You will learn information at these sessions that may be difficult to find elsewhere.

Administrators, staff, faculty, current students and other campus community members lead the orientation sessions and present first hand advice. These people are the best sources of preliminary information. In addition, many of these people will serve as resources later on, if a question or problem arises. **GET THEIR NAMES, PHONE NUMBERS, EMAIL ADDRESSES, AND OFFICE LOCATIONS.**

Faculty involved with the orientation sessions have typically worked at the school for many years, even decades. They know about different classes, degrees available, requirements for graduation and other academic issues. They will often give details about tutoring, explain where to find the writing center, and describe other academic services.

Members of student government, resident assistants, student advisors, and other student leaders will run additional portions of new student orientations. Students who run the orientation sessions usually give a tour of the campus, which helps to familiarize you with the buildings and to figure out key locations. These students are an invaluable resource since they have recently experienced being a new student and will know more about what you are going through than anyone else on campus. They can answer questions about extracurricular activities, student groups and any other non-academic opportunities.

> STAFF MEMBERS WILL BE YOUR RESOURCE FOR TECHNOLOGY HELP, INTERNSHIP OPPORTUNITIES, CAREER SERVICES, AND OTHER SUPPORT ACTIVITY.

Staff members include librarians, health workers, coaches and other non-faculty members who play an important role at your college. They will be your resource for technology help, internship opportunities, career services, and other support activity. They will help you when you get sick, need help with your email account, or any other support service.

Some of these staff members will lead sessions about costs, expenses, loans, and other issues related to the financial part of college. Others will explain how to use technology specific to the college and where the best Wi-Fi spots are.

WHAT TO EXPECT

A Pleasant Atmosphere

College campuses are among the nicest places on earth. They are typically attractive, well maintained and designed to generate a pleasant feel. Apple,

Facebook, Google, now Alphabet, and other companies have designed their corporate headquarters to look and feel like college campuses. Young adults walking, talking, playing games and socializing in green, manicured courtyards generate an energetic, exciting atmosphere. Interesting cafes, restaurants, and stores are often strategically located nearby. On many campuses, continuous entertainments and activities create a vibrant and unique culture.

Friendly People

Many new students are surprised at the pleasant attitudes they encounter on campus. Remember, colleges exist to serve you, and the majority of campus employees enjoy being helpful. If you need something, just ask. Ask and keep asking.

Fun

Campuses hold regularly sponsored events such as lectures, films, athletic events, intramural sports, plays, art exhibitions, and comedy shows. Many clubs and organizations also sponsor formal and informal activities, such as the Spanish club's Cinco de Mayo party.

College settings offer something for everyone, so it's even easier to make friends than it was in high school. There are opportunities to get to know all kinds of people at clubs, dorms, social events and in classes. It may take a little time but you will find people with different or similar interests who will become friends.

GENERAL DIFFERENCES BETWEEN HIGH SCHOOL AND COLLEGE

Greater Freedom, More Responsibility

In college if you are living away from home, nobody is constantly observing you. You may have a friend from high school or an older sibling keeping tabs on you, but likely you will mostly be on your own. This is good and bad. It gives you the opportunity to do a lot, but it also gives you the opportunity to do very little. Losing the support structure of family and high school friends can be a major adjustment for many students. Remember there are people around you that will form a new group of friends. **GET INVOLVED IN CLUBS OR ACTIVITIES AS SOON AS YOU CAN.**

Your newfound freedom may cause uncertainty and trepidation at some point. College can be scary. You are away from familiar surroundings. It is natural to feel overwhelmed or intimidated at times. Keep in mind that everybody feels this way at one point or another. **YOU ARE NOT ALONE.** You may be worried about finding friends or being on your own, but so is everybody else. Try one club, if it is not for you, try another. **YOU WILL FIND YOUR NICHE.**

Challenges Navigating the System

It is typically easy to find your way around a campus, even large ones, with maps and apps for your cell phone. But it is often hard to know some of the basic information about what you are supposed to do, when you are supposed to do it and how you should do it. Most colleges don't have a central authority that has information about the requirements for your major, where to sign up for intramural sports, how to get a night shift on the college radio station or what to do to get into a closed class. It can be difficult to get answers to even the simplest questions. There is always somebody to help; there will be somebody who knows the answer to your question. **ASK AND KEEP ASKING.** Ask your student guide, your resident assistant or faculty advisor. If they do not know they can point you to somebody who does.

Less Structure than High School

High school requires students to physically be there from a certain time in the morning to a certain time in the afternoon. There is a typical routine that is followed most days. In college, for the most part you can take classes when you want (classes often start at 8 am and go until 10 pm). **FIND A ROUTINE THAT WORKS FOR YOU.**

More Choices When Picking Classes

College offers more choices; in many cases you can decide what courses you want to take, what day and time to take the class, in which semester you'll take the course, and which professor you want to take. While some schools make advising mandatory, advice can be poor or non-existent at others. You may have to seek out advisors or professors to make sure you are taking the right courses. (This will be covered in more detail in Chapter 7.)

A Multitude of Potential Majors

Many times the major you start with is not the major you end up with. Students come into college having picked a major because of a good high school teacher, potential for a good job, their uncle works in the field, or a host of other reasons. After taking a few classes in a major, some students find that they are no longer interested or that they prefer another field. **DON'T BE AFRAID TO CHANGE YOUR MIND.**

Feeling Overwhelmed

Arrival on campus can leave you bombarded with so much so fast. Immediately you have to deal with a new living arrangement, register, attend classes, find your way around, and meet people. **BREAK THINGS INTO SMALL COMPONENTS AND DEAL WITH THEM ONE AT A TIME.**

Copious Free Time

On average a typical student takes 15 credit hours of classes during each semester. 15 credit hours means you spend 15 hours in class each week. By not spending as much time in the classroom as you did in high school, it is easy to think that you have more time than you do. It can be easy to get lazy. **SET BLOCKS OF TIME ASIDE TO STUDY AND IMMEDIATELY COMPLETE TASKS.**

Institutional Priorities

The sole purpose of a high school is to teach high school students. The primary focus of some universities, however, is to conduct research and to educate graduate students. This does not mean they do not care about teaching undergraduates, it's just that you are not always their top priority.

Differences Between High School and College Classes

Graded Material

You are now independent and will be expected to be responsible for your getting your college work done. High schools give regular homework, in-class exercises, quizzes and shorter assignments. This is not the case in college. Most grades are based primarily on just a few tests and papers per semester. Because there is less graded homework involved, **you need to spend a lot more time doing work on your own and realize that there will be fewer opportunities to be graded.**

> It is easy to put off required reading until the night before an exam. Don't fall into the "night before" trap!

The emphasis on tests and papers means there are fewer opportunities to show how well or to discover how poorly, you are doing. In some cases two or three tests comprise your entire grade. You may start class at the beginning of September, but not take your first test until the middle of October. It is easy to put off required reading until the night before the exam. Trying to learn six weeks of material in one night isn't easy. One of the biggest surprises for students is the large amount of material covered on tests. Don't fall into the "night before" trap!

Personal Responsibility

High school is required, college is not. In high school, teachers take attendance and may inquire if a student misses class or ask if something is wrong, if they notice your grades drop considerably. In college you are much more likely to fall through the cracks. Professors assume you are there because you want to be. If you don't show up for class, no one is calling home. The freedom to sleep late, stay and chat with friends or otherwise not show up at class without anyone looking over your shoulder is an easy habit to get into. **Develop the habit of thinking that class is required even if it is not.** It also might help to think about how much you or your parents are paying to attend each class. Don't waste your money!

Classes are Less Structured

High school classes tend to be more structured than college classes. In high school there are lesson plans the teachers have to follow and guidelines for what material has to be covered. Sometimes in college classes you will bounce from topic to topic. This makes taking notes more difficult and more essential. Though most classes have to cover specific material, college professors tend to have freer reign over their methods and material.

Classes are More Difficult

At first it may seem like college is a breeze, with no daily or weekly assignments to turn in. Don't be misled. You are expected to work independently. In addition, many students make the mistake of thinking they can get by with doing the same amount of studying that they did in high school. You most likely cannot. There is enormous variability in how well high schools prepare students for college. **PLAN TO STUDY DAILY**. In college, typically there is less emphasis on memorizing and repeating material and more emphasis on critical thinking and synthesizing ideas. This can be a difficult adjustment for many students. In your first year especially, **IT IS BETTER TO BE OVER PREPARED THAN UNDER PREPARED**.

Some first-year students do not think they are learning information or skills that they will use specifically for their jobs in the future. Don't be disappointed. It may not be immediately apparent. In contrast, technical degrees usually train individuals to do a specific job. Many two-year colleges provide technical degrees. Training in a specific field teaches you a certain skill. For some students a technical degree is preferable.

Classes are Longer and Larger

College classes may last anywhere from 55 minutes to three hours. Depending on the school and the course, college class sizes may range anywhere from 12 to over 250 students. Introductory classes at large universities are notorious for having huge numbers of students. Learning to handle larger class sizes can be a major adjustment for many new college students.

Classes are Fast Paced

You will be expected to cover college-level material much more quickly than you did high school lessons. So it can be easy to fall behind. Many classes meet only twice a week, so if you skip one class you have missed a half a week of material. A question worth 15 or 20 percent of your test may have been covered that day. If you miss a class, be sure to get notes from a classmate so that you don't miss out on critical information.

Time Moves Quickly

Because classes are less structured and more informal with less supervision, it is easy to slack off. This is especially true early in the term when there are no assignments due. Before you know it, you may be a month or more behind in your work. Exacerbating this is the way the semesters are structured. Usually tests, projects, presentations and papers are due at times bunched together in the middle of the semester and at the end. **START EARLY ON PAPERS, PROJECTS AND OTHER ASSIGNMENTS SO THAT YOU CAN SPREAD OUT YOUR WORK OVER A LONGER PERIOD OF TIME.** You don't want to be writing a ten page paper the same night you are studying for a final exam.

Usually Less Interaction with Teachers

Since classes are larger and meet less often, and you are expected to work independently and responsibly, there is usually less interaction between students and teachers. In fact, some classes are just lectures where the professor tells you what you need to know for the test and has teaching assistants for office hours, so there is not any opportunity for interaction.

A Lot of Variability in Professors

Some classes are very easy, others are extremely challenging. Some teachers expect very little and others expect an enormous amount of work. Some professors are great teachers and some are just horrible. **BE PREPARED FOR A RANGE IN QUALITY AND DIFFERENCES IN CLASSES AND TEACHERS.** Just because one professor acts and teaches in a certain way does not mean that all of them will be the same.

LIVING AWAY FROM HOME

As big as the adjustment from high school to college academics may be, living away from family and friends may prove just as challenging. For many students living away is the best, and for others, it's the scariest part of college.

New Experiences

There are lots of things you may encounter for the first time, including something as mundane as writing your first check, or signing up for a study abroad program. Living with a non-relative in a dorm can be trying for almost anyone. Because you will be doing so many things for the first time, you won't always do them perfectly. **RECOGNIZE THAT YOU WILL MAKE MISTAKES AND DON'T BE TOO HARD ON YOURSELF BECAUSE OF THEM.**

> THERE ARE LOTS OF THINGS YOU MAY ENCOUNTER FOR THE FIRST TIME…RECOGNIZE THAT YOU WILL OCCASIONALLY FEEL PRESSURED; BE STRONG AND TRUE TO YOURSELF.

Peer Pressure

Parents hope that by the time their kids get to college they are well adjusted individuals with a solid sense of identity with moral and ethical behavior. However, many students need their time at college to finish maturing. So you may tend to do things to be part of the crowd in order to fit in. Recognize that you will occasionally feel pressured; **BE STRONG AND BE TRUE TO YOURSELF.**

Independence

Parents today are more involved with their children than previous generations. Most parents of today's college students have been very active in planning activities for their kids, and of course helping them choose a college. **COLLEGE IS A GREAT TIME TO DO MORE FOR YOU.** Rely on your parents, but start making your own decisions.

There is no magic bullet, there is nothing to completely prepare you. Being away from home is extremely difficult for many people. It is a great time to assert your independence, to learn who you are. Do new things, try something you normally wouldn't. But make smart, good choices. **MAKE THE MOST OF YOUR NEW-FOUND INDEPENDENCE AND FREEDOM.**

REMEMBER...

GET INVOLVED IN CLUBS OR ACTIVITIES AS SOON AS YOU CAN. YOU WILL FIND YOUR NICHE.

BREAK THINGS INTO SMALL COMPONENTS AND DEAL WITH THEM ONE AT A TIME.

SET BLOCKS OF TIME ASIDE TO STUDY AND IMMEDIATELY COMPLETE TASKS.

PLAN TO STUDY DAILY. IT IS BETTER TO BE OVER PREPARED THAN UNDER PREPARED.

BE PREPARED FOR A RANGE IN QUALITY AND DIFFERENCES IN CLASSES AND TEACHERS.

RECOGNIZE THAT YOU WILL MAKE MISTAKES AND DON'T BE TOO HARD ON YOURSELF BECAUSE OF THEM.

chapter 5
TYPES OF CLASSES

O ne of the most common reasons students do not complete their degree in four years is that they are unaware of the specific requirements. Students often take classes they don't need or that don't count toward graduation. **THIS CHAPTER TELLS YOU HOW TO TAKE CLASSES STRATEGICALLY, SO THAT YOU CAN FINISH IN FOUR YEARS.** (Or less if you come into college with credit for AP classes.)

The majority of college degrees require completion of 120 credit hours to graduate (engineering and a few other majors require more). Most classes are three credit hours. Thus, you will need to take approximately 40 classes. Most colleges have two semesters during the year so in order to graduate in four years, you need to average five classes (15 credit hours) each semester for eight semesters. Some classes, usually science, have laboratory sessions and provide more credit hours. The number of credit hours for music, art, theater, and physical education classes varies.

When you enter a college as a first-year or transfer student you will be assigned to a particular catalogue for that academic year. The catalogue provides information about majors, minors and classes available and the requirements that you must meet in order to graduate. It will be a paper booklet or electronic (on a specific site on the website) or both.

All schools have precise, unique requirements, broad categories of classes that must be taken. Spend time reading your catalogue so you know what types of majors and classes are available. **AS YOU TAKE CLASSES, MAKE SURE YOU KNOW WHAT CATEGORIES THEY FIT INTO SO THAT YOU MEET THE SPECIFIC REQUIREMENTS FOR YOUR MAJOR AND THE COLLEGE.**

Requirements for graduation sometimes change from year to year. **Be sure to follow your catalogue for your academic year, class and major**. Be aware that some of your required classes may not be offered every semester, or even every year, so in some situations you need to plan ahead a year or more in advance. Sometimes courses have to be taken in order; the first is a pre-requisite for the next.

The catalogue gives you information about graduation requirements; the course schedule tells you what classes are offered each semester. The course schedule

> **Broadly, there are four categories of classes: general education classes, classes in your major and minor, special college requirements, and electives.**

is provided on the Website or published in a booklet every year or semester before classes start. The schedule will also provide information about who is teaching the class, the time and place it is offered, and other relevant items.

Broadly there are four categories of classes. General education classes are required by almost all colleges. Classes in your major and minor are required for your specific degree. Special college requirements are specific classes that are unique for each different institution. Electives are classes without any restrictions that do not count towards general education or your major, but do count towards the 120 credit hours. In addition, you can have two or more majors, and/or minors. **Most (if not all) classes you take every semester should fulfill the requirements for the first three categories.**

Pick classes strategically. For example, **there are some classes that fulfill the requirements for your major AND also count towards general education.** An introductory Economics class will likely fulfill the social science requirement in general education and also fulfill a required class for an accounting major. In other cases there are classes that fulfill requirements for two different majors so it is easier to graduate with a double major. **Double dip to fill requirements whenever you can.**

YOUR OFFICIAL TRANSCRIPT IS KEPT BY THE REGISTRAR'S OFFICE, WHICH RECORDS CLASSES YOU HAVE TAKEN. You can check with the registrar's office at any time to find out what requirements remain unfilled. You will also have access to your transcript through the college's website. Make sure you know what is on your transcript at all times. Be sure to ask a faculty advisor or go to the advising center if you are not clear about what is necessary to fulfill requirements. The rest of this chapter will explain the four broad categories, levels and types of classes.

GENERAL EDUCATION REQUIREMENTS

General education (Gen Ed) requirements are specific classes within broad categories that are required for all students getting a Bachelor of Arts (BA) or Bachelor of Science (BS) degree. Typically a BA places more emphasis on the Humanities and a BS requires more quantitative classes. Approximately one-quarter to one-third of the classes needed to graduate are general education courses. General education classes consist of—composition, math, humanities, social sciences and natural sciences.

To fulfill general education requirements you have to take a certain number of classes in different categories. Within the categories there is often a lot of flexibility. For example, you may be required to take two social science classes. The social sciences include economics, political science, psychology, sociology and more, so you have many options. In addition, within a discipline, you may have the option of taking classes that focus on family, different cultures, adolescence and many other topics. Given that YOU HAVE CHOICES, TAKE CLASSES THAT INTEREST YOU.

Make sure you are aware of all the options you have. The number of classes within the categories has expanded dramatically over the past few decades. Twenty years ago to fulfill the humanities requirement a student would only have a few choices about different literature classes. Now there are classes about movies, music and even comic books that fulfill the humanities requirement at many schools. TAKE AT LEAST ONE CLASS YOU REALLY LIKE EVERY SEMESTER. It helps to have something to look forward to.

Though the number of credit hours in each category varies, all colleges require some Gen Ed classes. In general these classes are easier to transfer to other schools than other types of classes. The basic Gen Ed classes, such as Introduction to Microeconomics, are easy to transfer – esoteric classes, such as Lady Gaga in Music, are not.

SPECIFIC COLLEGE REQUIREMENTS

Many schools require certain classes for graduation that can be taken only at their institution. The classes may be treated as credit towards a degree at another college but don't fulfill a requirement. They are called something along the lines of special university classes, other college requirements, core classes or all-college requirements. Ethics, globalization, sustainability and cross disciplinary study have increased in importance over the past decade. Most colleges have responded to this by requiring students to take classes developed by their college in these areas. **IN SOME CASES THESE CLASSES ALSO FULFILL GEN ED REQUIREMENTS, SO YOU CAN DOUBLE DIP BY HAVING ONE OF THESE CLASSES MEET TWO REQUIREMENTS.**

In addition, some colleges have language, religion or other specific requirements. Some colleges within a university may also have additional courses that students in other colleges at the same university do not need to take. Be aware of any special required classes.

MAJOR REQUIREMENTS

Your major is the area in which you specialize. You take most of your classes from this discipline. Most majors require between 30 and 50 credit hours. Each major requires specific courses, but usually also allows choices, such as being able to pick one of three classes from a particular area. In these situations, take classes that interest you or from a professor you like.

Some colleges in a university have standards that must be met before you can officially declare a major and enter that college. For example, at some universities you have to take introductory accounting and economics classes before you can officially get into the business school and declare yourself a management major. In addition, some majors require a certain Grade Point Average (GPA) for a set number of credit hours before you can officially declare that major.

Some students think that once they declare a certain major they are going to work in that discipline the rest of their life. Some students are timid about picking a major, because they feel they will be 'stuck' in that area forever. **MOST PEOPLE CHANGE CAREERS (NOT JOBS) AT LEAST THREE TIMES DURING THEIR LIVES.** In addition, with jobs during college, internships, classes and independent study, you can tailor your resume to a specific job, company, industry or area. Nonetheless, **PICK A MAJOR YOU LIKE.**

MINOR REQUIREMENTS

A minor in a discipline requires fewer credit hours than a major and usually does not entail as many upper level classes. It is intended to provide students with minimum competency in an area. You can minor in an area that relates to your major (for example an Economics minor fits with a Finance major) or in something that interests you.

A MINOR IN AN UNRELATED AREA CAN ALSO COMPLEMENT MANY MAJORS. A business minor is a good idea for an art major who wants to set up their own studio. Basically they will be running their own business and knowing the basics of accounting and marketing will help them be successful in their chosen endeavor. An art minor is a great idea for a marketing major to help them think about things in a creative way. Talk with professors or professionals in the area; there are many relationships between disciplines that are not readily apparent.

ELECTIVES

For most degrees, two-thirds to three-quarters of the classes you take fulfill requirements for general education, your major and the university. Then you have ten or more classes with the freedom to take anything you want to finish the 120 credit hours. These are typically among the best classes, because you can indulge your interests. Electives are often classes professors have developed from their personal interests, thus their enthusiasm can make practically any topic fascinating.

TAKE CLASSES THAT FIT YOUR PERSONALITY. What interests you? What do you want to know more about? Here is your opportunity to explore. IF, HOWEVER, YOU WANT TO BE PRACTICAL, TAKE CLASSES THAT FIT YOUR FUTURE GOALS. If you are planning on attending law school and are majoring in Political Science, take Economics classes. If you are most concerned about your career, take classes you think will help you land your ideal job.

BE CAREFUL WITH SOME TYPES OF ELECTIVE COURSES. The number of credit hours counted as electives that can be applied towards graduation is often capped for certain classes. For example, you can only take a certain number of physical education courses that count towards your degree.

LEVELS AND TYPES OF CLASSES

Undergraduate classes are numbered from the 100s to the 400s. Typically classes numbered 500 and above are graduate classes. In some situations a class is listed as both 400 and 500 so seniors and graduate students can both take it for credit. There are also remedial classes numbered below 100 that must be taken by some students before a 100 level class. Typically these classes are for students who lack proficiency in a certain area. REMEDIAL CLASSES DO NOT COUNT TOWARDS THE 120 CREDIT HOURS NEEDED FOR GRADUATION. The lower-level classes, generally numbered 100 and 200, are typically an introduction and/or overview of a topic. These classes are intended for first-year students and sophomores; the 300 and 400 level classes are for juniors and seniors.

Lower-Level Classes

Though the material in the upper-level classes is usually more difficult, the lower-level classes are in some ways harder. Remember, many students will flunk out and they typically do so while taking these classes. The preparation of students in introductory-level classes can vary dramatically. Some students are struggling to keep up while others find the class too easy. The classes are often mandatory for certain requirements so some of the students do not want to be there.

The lower-level classes are often taught by the least experienced teachers. Typically, not always, these classes are assigned to the newest faculty members. Also, at large universities graduate students (Teaching Assistants or TAs) often teach many first-year students' level classes. And at many colleges, adjunct (part-time) faculty teach a large percentage of the introductory-level classes.

In addition, finding courses to take as you attempt to fulfill requirements can be challenging. First-year students register last. Upper classmen have priority and they know who the better teachers are. So, first-year students may be stuck with classes they aren't excited about or classes taught by the least popular teachers. Don't be discouraged. Remember, if you can make it through the first semester or two, you'll begin to have higher priority in choosing classes, and you can make it to the end.

Generally, introductory classes are larger than upper-level classes. They tend to be in a lecture format and grades are mainly based on tests. In some cases, a professor will lecture twice a week and a graduate student will lead discussion sessions to answer questions and clarify material.

> FINDING COURSES TO TAKE AS YOU ATTEMPT TO FULFILL REQUIREMENTS CAN BE CHALLENGING. FIRST-YEAR STUDENTS REGISTER LAST...IF YOU CAN MAKE IT THROUGH THE FIRST FEW SEMESTERS, YOU'LL BEGIN TO HAVE HIGHER PRIORITY IN CHOOSING CLASSES.

Upper-Level Classes

The 300 and 400 upper-level classes offer more in-depth material within a discipline. Some upper-level classes are open to all students; but most 300 or 400 level classes require students to be a junior or a senior. In addition, many of the upper-level classes are sequential: there are pre-requisites courses you must take. **SO IF YOU NEED OR WANT TO TAKE A CERTAIN 300 OR 400 LEVEL CLASS, MAKE SURE YOU PLAN YOUR SCHEDULE WELL IN ADVANCE SO THAT YOU TAKE THE REQUIRED 100 AND/OR 200 LEVEL CLASSES FIRST.**

Upper-level classes are usually smaller, have more student participation, and allow more interaction with the professor. These classes are usually taught by full-time faculty, who are experts in the subject matter and whose enthusiasm about the topic becomes contagious. In general there are fewer tests, but longer papers, debates, discussions, student presentations, and other active forms of assessment.

Independent Study

In addition to classes listed in the catalogue, you have the option to develop a special topics class in an area that interests you. If there isn't a class offered on something you want to learn, you just need to find a professor knowledgeable in that area to supervise your project.

In your catalogue there will be courses listed under most majors as Independent Study. These are variable credit hour classes, meaning that the larger and more time consuming your project, the more credit hours you will receive for completing it.

Small Group or Individual Research Classes

Most colleges have opportunities for undergraduate research where students will work one-on-one or in small groups with a professor. Here students learn how to test hypotheses, collect data, conduct experiments and otherwise apply unique approaches to learning. This is a great way to prepare for graduate school or for many careers.

Internships

Internships give academic credit for working at an organization. You will also need a professor or staff member to supervise the internship and write a paper or complete another academic project describing your work experience. Check with the career center at your college for opportunities and specific requirements. Some internships are paid while others are not. The number of credit hours you get towards graduation varies by the specific internship, the number of hours worked, the amount of time you meet with your faculty supervisor and the scope of the academic project.

Internships are a great way to explore a company, job, industry or discipline. They provide a way for you to determine if you have an interest in something. It is a relatively easy, low cost, low time commitment way to expose yourself to different opportunities. It also looks great on a resume and can provide opportunities for future jobs.

Virtual Classes

Many professors are increasingly using technology in their classes. Power point slides are used for lectures, grades are posted on-line and emails are used to communicate with students. Some classes are hybrid, requiring both in-person class meetings and on-line discussions or quizzes.

Classes that are taught completely on-line, where there is no face-to-face interaction between students and the professor, are part of the curriculum at many colleges. Distance education classes can be a great way to fill in a Gen Ed requirement or other necessary class. There is an enormous degree of variability in the quality of these classes; so do not necessarily avoid them, but be wary.

Study Abroad Programs

A wonderful way to expose yourself to new things, expand your horizons and set yourself apart from your peers is to participate in a study abroad program. You can spend a semester living and taking classes at a school in another country. You do not necessarily need to know another language to participate.

The international programs department will have information on the countries where you can study, the number of credit hours you will earn, and which classes taken abroad will count towards Gen Ed or towards your major. Plan your study abroad as soon as possible to make sure you finish any required classes before you leave and that the classes you take at a college in another country count towards your degree.

OTHER CLASSES FOR CREDIT

In addition to the standard format where students and professors meet in a classroom, there are also classes for credit that are structured differently. Some majors, such as education, require students to engage in teaching in their area at an elementary school or high school. Radio labs, field work for sciences and classes in theater are some examples from other fields.

REMEMBER...

TAKE AT LEAST ONE CLASS YOU REALLY LIKE
EVERY SEMESTER.

PEOPLE CHANGE CAREERS (NOT JOBS)
AT LEAST THREE TIMES DURING THEIR LIVES...
PICK A MAJOR YOU LIKE.

A MINOR IN AN UNRELATED AREA CAN
COMPLIMENT MANY MAJORS.

TAKE ELECTIVE CLASSES THAT FIT YOUR
PERSONALITY AND/OR YOUR FUTURE GOALS.

IF YOU NEED OR WANT TO TAKE AN UPPER-LEVEL
CLASS, MAKE SURE YOU PLAN YOUR SCHEDULE WELL
IN ADVANCE SO THAT YOU TAKE THE REQUIRED
LOWER-LEVEL CLASSES FIRST.

chapter 6
PEOPLE

ADVISORS

Before you start college, an advisor will help you pick classes for your first semester or year. This person will be a staff member who is a professional advisor, a graduate student, or a faculty member. This person may be temporary, just helping you get started, or they could be your advisor until you graduate. **If your advisor is temporary, find a permanent advisor as soon as possible, preferably in your major.** The more time you spend with one person, the better they will know you and the more prepared they will be to help you. Use your advisor to help you pick classes, making sure you fulfill all your requirements, find internships if possible and help you with other academic aspects.

If your advisor is a faculty member, select someone from your major department. Then your advisor will be able to help guide you in your academic requirements and then towards your future career. They may have contacts at companies, may know what graduate schools fit your needs and can describe what to expect in your field.

While your advisor will help you select classes, **you need to know what is required.** Advisors are not perfect, they may occasionally miss something or make a mistake. In addition, you know yourself better than they do. They may pick classes for you that you do not like or pick times that are bad for you. **You need to know your catalogue and course schedule and pick your classes before meeting with your advisor.**

TEACHING FACULTY

Most college professors have PhDs (Doctor of Philosophy), a degree that usually takes between four and seven years beyond a Bachelor's Degree to complete. A PhD is a terminal degree meaning that it is the highest level of schooling an individual can receive.[12] To be accredited, colleges usually need a certain number of faculty with PhDs.[13] If a teacher does not have a PhD they are not referred to as "doctor."

Professors can be broadly classified into: tenured or tenure track versus non-tenure track and full-time or part-time. In general, though not always, assistant, associate, and full professors are full-time and tenured or tenure track while teaching assistants, instructors (lecturers), and adjunct faculty are part-time and non-tenure track. It is the full-time tenured faculty that control the curriculum and other academic areas that students must follow.

TYPES OF PROFESSORS

Professors

Typically, older faculty, (full) professors have been at their institution ten years or more. They have earned tenure and have a large degree of job security.[14] There are certain benefits and costs of being in only one place for a long period of time. Professors enjoy their subjects and find teaching young adults rewarding. They know the curriculum well, so they can be great resources when it comes to questions about graduation requirements and other areas in the college. On the other hand, sometimes teachers can get a little too set in their ways and become rigid in their methods.

Associate Professors

Associate professors have tenure, some of these professors as Assistant professors spent so much time doing everything non-teaching related necessary to

---

12 There are a few exceptions to this. In some disciplines an individual can get a post-doctorate. This is usually done by people engaging in a very specific area of research. There are also EdDs (Doctor of Education) and DBAs Doctor of Business Administration). Most fine arts terminal degrees are not PhDs.

13 Accreditation bodies are government agencies that evaluate a post-secondary institution's mission and ensure it meets all necessary standards for providing the educational (and other) services.

14 Tenure is an appointment where the teacher cannot be dismissed from their job without just cause. It is intended to provide academic freedom and continuity. It is somewhat controversial though because some argue that it can lead to complacency.

get tenure that they did not have much time available for students. Sometimes, particularly at research universities, Associate professors feel guilty about not having spent lots of time on their teaching during the first part of their career so they work at it harder at this point. Having job security allows Associate professors the luxury of being able to spend their time on what they like. Most professors like teaching and working with young adults and are reinvigorated at the prospect of doing a better job as a teacher.

Assistant Professors

Most assistant professors have recently (the previous one to six years) earned their PhD. Generally they are the youngest faculty members, are relatively new to the college and do not have as much experience teaching. They can also be more energetic and in touch with students because they are closest in terms of age and experiences. At research universities assistant professors spend their time trying to get tenure by conducting research, not by teaching. They can often be stressed and distracted, though they can still be highly competent teachers.

Teaching Assistants

A significant proportion of students at national universities are graduate students. These are also the people who teach many of the undergraduate classes. In exchange for tuition and a small stipend, graduate students work for the university conducting research or teaching classes. Graduate students typically teach the introductory classes. They are new to the classroom and their focus tends to be on the classes they are taking and on completing their dissertation. Typically, though not always, they are not the best teachers, not because they do not want to be but because they do not have the experience or the time to spend to be a good teacher.

Instructors, Lecturers, and Adjunct Professors

Due to cuts in state budgets for higher education many colleges and universities are relying more on part-time faculty to teach classes. The primary reason is cost; part-time teachers are less expensive than full time faculty. **THERE IS A LOT OF VARIABILITY IN THE QUALITY OF INSTRUCTORS.** Typically their job is to only teach so they usually do not participate in advising, curriculum changes or any other college decisions. They often teach as many, or more, classes as full-time faculty. Because their focus is solely on teaching, they can be very good.

Adjunct professors are typically hired on a course-to-course basis. The adjunct professors are also hit or miss. **IN SOME CASES, THESE PART-TIME PROFESSORS CAN BE EXCELLENT. THEY TEACH A CLASS OR TWO A YEAR BECAUSE THEY ENJOY IT OR THEY ARE EXPERTS IN A CERTAIN AREA.** Lawyers, engineers, and other professionals have experience that most college professors do not. Students can learn a lot from these experts.

IN OTHER SITUATIONS, THOUGH, BE WARY OF ADJUNCT PROFESSORS. Some of them try to make a living as an adjunct, they may teach at four or five schools to try and make ends meet. They may be too busy or too harried, driving from place to place, and don't have time to put into their classes.

Staff

Course schedules list the classes, days, and times of the week that they meet, and the professor teaching the class. Sometimes there will be spots for professors listed as "staff." This means that when the classes were put into the schedule there was no professor assigned to teach it. Typically teaching assistants, instructors, or adjunct professors are assigned to teach these classes at a later date. Full-time professors choose the classes they will teach, then staff cover the least desirable classes in terms of time and/or material. Be wary of who may be teaching a class where the teacher is staff.

OTHER FACULTY

Administration

The administration runs the college. Administration includes vice-presidents, deans, associate deans, heads of student affairs, and other student services filled by non-teaching personnel. The person in administration that most students would have some kind of contact is the Dean of Students (or someone else in their office, such as an assistant dean). These administrators can be a source of great support. **MANY PEOPLE IN ADMINISTRATION WILL OFTEN BE YOUR BIGGEST ADVOCATES.**

Support Staff

Support staff, such as department secretaries, helps run the college on a day-to-day basis. Most of these people, in addition to being knowledgeable about the college, are very friendly and can be your ally. They often know about closed classes or added sections of courses, and can sometimes help with scheduling problems.

Coaches

If you play a sport, coaches can help you navigate the system, serve as allies, and provide support.

Students

Some students also play a role in the operation of a college. This includes Resident Assistants, orientation leaders, and student government leaders. Most, if not all, of these students will assist new students who need help. These students are more familiar with certain aspects of the college than faculty and staff. They especially know the unwritten rules of how to navigate college. **GET TO KNOW THESE STUDENT LEADERS—THEY ARE AN INVALUABLE SOURCE OF HELP.**

REMEMBER...

IF YOUR ADVISOR IS TEMPORARY, FIND A PERMANENT ADVISOR ASAP, PREFERABLY IN YOUR MAJOR.

YOU NEED TO KNOW YOUR CATALOGUE AND COURSE SCHEDULE AND PICK YOUR CLASSES BEFORE MEETING WITH YOUR ADVISOR.

MANY PEOPLE IN ADMINISTRATION WILL OFTEN BE YOUR BIGGEST ADVOCATES.

GET TO KNOW STUDENT LEADERS—THEY ARE AN INVALUABLE SOURCE OF HELP.

chapter 7
TIPS FOR SUCCESS

COLLEGES AND UNIVERSITIES WANT YOU TO SUCCEED! The president, deans, and other administrators want you to attend and stay to graduate because it enhances their image in the rankings, to parents, and to peer institutions. Professors want you to succeed because they enjoy seeing young individuals learn, grow, and prosper.

STARTING OUT

Be Inquisitive

START COLLEGE BY ASKING QUESTIONS. Be curious about other people, new opportunities, and your surroundings. College presents a great opportunity to develop your intellectual curiosity. There are so many things to learn in and out of the classroom. Ask, "What if…? Why? What about this?" The willingness to learn is as important as what you learn.

Curiosity will be beneficial throughout your life. At a job, if you ask questions like: "How does this work?" or "What are the impacts of this decision?" and maybe "Is there a better way to do this?" or "Why is this done this way?" then you learn much more about what you are doing. You learn not only what your immediate job is, but also what other coworkers do, how the organization operates, and potentially how improvements can be made. Workers who know more about what they and those around them are doing tend to be promoted faster and have more opportunities than those who do not.

In addition to asking questions about the college, classes, and other people, ASK QUESTIONS ABOUT YOURSELF. What interests me? What classes in the course catalogue appeal most to me? Why do I like this particular class or professor? Find out what kind of student and person you are. If you can figure out why you like certain topics, activities, and classes, it will help you pick a major, find a satisfying career, and make life choices that can lead to happiness.

Be Realistic and Be Honest with Yourself

Get to know yourself. Some of us go through our lives making promises we do not keep; we don't live up to the often unrealistic goals we set for ourselves (such as getting up at 5 am to exercise every day before work). The trend can start in college. **SET GOALS, STRIVE TO BE BETTER, BUT BE REALISTIC.**

Some students go into college thinking, "I did not work very hard in high school, but now that I am in college I will." Then they register for hard classes, get bogged down, frustrated, struggle and flunk out. **WORK TO IMPROVE YOURSELF, BUT MAKE CHANGES GRADUALLY;** you are much more likely to obtain your goals if they are realistic.

> FIND OUT WHAT KIND OF STUDENT AND PERSON YOU ARE. IF YOU CAN FIGURE OUT WHY YOU LIKE CERTAIN TOPICS, ACTIVITIES, AND CLASSES, IT WILL HELP YOU PICK A MAJOR, FIND A SATISFYING CAREER, AND MAKE LIFE CHOICES THAT CAN LEAD TO HAPPINESS.

Don't Focus (too much) on the Future

Part of the reason you are attending college is to get a good job. So it is hard to not worry about the future. There may be pressure on you to only take classes that count towards your major or other college requirements. You may feel you have to take a large number of credit hours to ensure that you graduate on time. You will also be asked (over and over and over), "What is your major?" or "What job are you going to get with that degree?" or "Why are you studying that?"

Having goals such as finishing required classes as quickly as possible, graduating on time and finding a good job are important. However, it is **MORE IMPORTANT FOR YOU TO BECOME ACCLIMATED TO COLLEGE**, get used to college level classes and to adjust to being on your own. As hard as it may be, don't worry too much about a major and future jobs your first year.

Accept Responsibility

At college, perhaps for the first time in your life, you will be expected to be an adult. Take responsibility for yourself and for your actions. Don't make excuses or blame others for what you do. If you make a mistake, admit it. Realize that it is up to you to meet deadlines for papers, tests and complete all other assignments.

Don't Be (too) Dumb

Mistakes are inevitable. If you are a typical college student, occasionally you will stay up late, oversleep, maybe drink too much, play loud music—the list is endless. Be careful. If you are going to drink, don't drive. If you are going to stay up all night during the week, you may miss your classes. One of the expectations of college students is that you are going to make mistakes. Don't be really dumb. Realize there are consequences for your actions. There is no one to blame but yourself. Accept responsibility and move on. Do better next time.

Be Careful with Technology

You have already posted material on Facebook, Twitter and other social media sites, taken photos of yourself and friends doing things you should not necessarily be doing, or sent a message saying something you regret. With technology keeping a digital record of all your activities, you need to be careful that there is not a record of something that a potential employer or other people would find disturbing.

Organization

Phones, PDAs, and planners are essential to keep you functioning effectively. You need to know how to plan your days and keep track of assignments and assessments. Plan specific days and times to complete papers, work on group projects and study for tests. Some professors won't give reminders about upcoming assignments but you are still responsible, so you need to stay on track on your own. **FIND AN ORGANIZATION SYSTEM THAT WORKS FOR YOU.**

TIPS ABOUT CLASSES BEFORE THE SEMESTER BEGINS

Learn the System Fast

Once or twice a year your college will put out a class schedule showing classes that are offered, the day and time each class meets, and which professor is teaching each class. Every college has a system for class registration based on class standing. Typically, upper classmen with more credit hours register for classes before lower classmen with fewer credit hours. **FIGURE OUT YOUR COLLEGE'S REGISTRATION SYSTEM IMMEDIATELY, AND SIGN UP AS EARLY AS POSSIBLE TO ENSURE YOU HAVE THE BEST POSSIBLE CHANCE TO GET THE CLASSES YOU WANT.**

Take Some Classes You Like Your First Semester/Year

You usually have the fewest options your first semester, but you still have some choices. **IF YOU LIKE THE CLASSES, IT IS LIKELY YOU WILL WANT TO ATTEND CLASS, DO THE REQUIRED READING, AND KEEP UP WITH THE ASSESSMENTS.** Take some general education classes and some classes in areas that interest you. This is not mutually exclusive – you will find classes that both satisfy college requirements and that you enjoy.

If you do poorly your first semester, getting Ds and Fs, you will be trying to catch up for at least the next year. You will be on academic probation, potentially leading to dismissal from the college. You will have to repeat any classes you fail. You will lose credit hours that count towards graduation. You will likely lose grants or other types of financial aid.

Find Out About Classes

Ask the professor about a course you're considering. Don't judge a book by its cover, you may think that physics will be boring and some other class will be exciting. The teacher often makes the class. You may be surprised that a calculus class is the best class you have had. **IF YOU ARE UNSURE ABOUT A FEW CLASSES, SIGN UP FOR AN EXTRA CLASS, THEN DROP THE ONE YOU DON'T LIKE.**

Be Aware of Class Size

Some classes are small with ten or fifteen students and others are very large with hundreds of students. Some people enjoy large classes where the only mode of teaching is in a lecture format. But many other students struggle in large classes where they are completely anonymous without personal attention.

Find a Workable Schedule

Since you have some control over the days and times you can take classes, determine what works best for you. If you have an hour or two between every class, do you spend your time on Facebook or do you use it to stay on top of your required reading? Is it better to have a have a few classes on Monday, Wednesday and Friday and a few on Tuesday and Thursday and study a little each day? Or is it better to have classes bunched together on a few days and spend the other days just studying?

For some students having classes all together helps so that they can set aside a large block of time for studying. For other students having classes spaced out so they can study in between classes is best. Create a schedule that works best for you.

Be Prepared for Difficult Courses

While colleges want you to succeed, there are some courses that are intended to be 'weed out' classes. For example, Organic Chemistry is meant to differentiate the serious premed students from everybody else, so professors routinely flunk many students. Steer clear of these classes your first year unless you are realistically prepared and have a reason to do so.

Take the Tough Classes From a Supportive Professor

Every subject area has difficult classes that may require extra attention. Every student will have courses that they will find more challenging. If there is an area you struggle with or a course you know will be hard for you, say math, find out which professors are most amenable to helping students.

If Possible, Avoid Classes with Common Exams

Many large schools have multiple sections of introductory classes every semester. Sometimes these exams are scheduled so that students from all sections take the test at the same time.

The common exams are sometimes made up by people other than the professor teaching your course section. If professors are teaching a class with common exams, they have to cover all of the material that will be on the exams. They may have to cover material that they don't like or may have to rush through topics quickly.

If you have to take a required class with common exams, take professors who have been teaching the class on a regular basis for a long time. They are familiar with how to teach the class, how to present the material you need to know, and how to prepare you better for the tests.

Use Email Appropriately

If you are going to contact a professor who does not know you, make sure you use email correctly. In the subject line put the class name and section number. Start with your name and the class. Next state the reason for the email as simply as possible. Then, put the onus of the situation on you, the student, not the professor and what needs to occur. Finish with what and how it can be completed.

(First Line)
Hello, Prof. _____ ,

(Second Part)
My name is _____ and I am/want to be/will be in _____ class in _____ term at _____ time.

(Third Part—state reason for the email)
I am on the waitlist for the class and want to make sure I can enroll.

(Fourth Part)
If you allow me to enroll, I will be in class the first day with the necessary forms for you to sign.

(End)
Thank you very much for your time.

TIPS FOR THE CLASSROOM

THE EXPECTATIONS PROFESSORS HAVE VARY EXTENSIVELY. There is a wide range in how professors approach teaching and grading. Some classes are easy, some very hard—sometimes the same class in a department. All professors have some minimum standard. You can fail the easiest class, if you don't do the work.

Attend Class

Attendance is not required for many classes. Sometimes the hardest part is just motivating yourself to go to class. Look for a reason (any reason) to attend class. For many courses, attendance is one of the top predictors of how well a student will do. Attending class is the best way to see what material the professor stresses and really helps you learn the difficult concepts.

> FOR MANY COURSES, ATTENDANCE IS ONE OF THE TOP PREDICTORS OF HOW WELL A STUDENT WILL DO OVERALL.

While professors do not like to flunk students, they do. It is much easier to give a low grade to somebody who does not show up for class on a regular basis. Not attending shows that the student does not care about the class. If the student does not care about the class, it is unlikely that the professor will care about the student or even know who they are.

Be On Time

It is usually the beginning of the class when professors remind students about upcoming assignments and answer questions from the previous class. Sometimes you won't be able to understand material later in the class session unless you know the material from the beginning of class.

Read the Syllabus Carefully!

Work smarter, not harder. **YOU NEED TO KNOW WHAT IS REWARDED AND FOCUS ON THOSE AREAS.** In college this means reading the syllabus carefully. Some students spend enormous amounts of time studying for a quiz that only comprises 10 percent of their grade, while spending almost no time on a project that was worth 30 percent of their grade.

The syllabus (see sample on next few pages) handed out the first day in class will tell you what determines your grade. **FOCUS ON THE ASSIGNMENTS THAT HAVE THE GREATEST IMPACT ON YOUR GRADE.**

Look at attendance, class requirements, and the percentage of each of the components for your grade. In some cases attendance is required and you lose points for missing class, in others it does not matter at all.

Requirements vary dramatically across disciplines. It can be as simple as only two tests in one class to a dozen different types of assignments in another. Obviously, spend the most time on the papers, projects, or tests that comprise the majority of your grade.

READ THE SYLLABUS CAREFULLY!

THE SYLLABUS HANDED OUT THE FIRST DAY OF EACH CLASS WILL TELL YOU WHAT DETERMINES YOUR GRADE.

REQUIREMENTS VARY DRAMATICALLY FROM CLASS TO CLASS.

Syllabus for a very important class
Course name and number
A very good college, term, and year
Department (Humanities, Science, etc.)

(Teacher Information)

Instructor: Doctor or Professor (Not Mr. or Mrs.)

Office: Where to go for help

Phone: Use only in an emergency

Email: Some professors love email and use it a lot, including answering questions from students, receiving papers and other assignments. Other professors use it but do not like to use it for their classes. The professor will tell you how much or how little to use it for their class.

Office Hours: These are the days and times that professors are guaranteed to be in their office to help students. If possible use these times to meet with your professor. (If you have other classes during this time, set up an appointment to meet the professor at another time.) Some professors have an open door policy where they are happy to see and help students any time they are in their office. Other professors will tell you to go away if you show up unannounced.

(Course Information)

Class Times: The time of day and days of the week that the class will meet.

Location: You need to know this before class starts; it will be in the class schedule, posted online and sometimes in print outside the department offices, registrar, or other easily found location.

Required Text(s):   Usually a very expensive book. If you purchase the book(s) from a website or somewhere other than the college bookstore, make sure it is the correct book and order it long before class starts. You will need it by the time class starts, sometimes before. Also, be sure that you have the correct edition. Even if it is the same book, old editions and international textbooks have different material and the order of the material may not be the same.

Optional Material: Sometimes a professor will recommend supplementary material. It is usually for math and other difficult classes.

Course Description: A course description provides an overview of the class. It may describe the material that will be covered during the semester and possibly how the class relates to other classes at the college.

Course Objective: A course objective describes what the professor wants the students to learn in the class. It can be basic, such as learning how to write better. It can be broad and esoteric, such as how the Crimean war impacts U.S. policy on terrorism today.

COURSE REQUIREMENTS:

Course Expectations: Different professors have different—sometimes very different—expectations. Do not assume that because one professor requires something that all do. Some professors require attendance for every class; others could care less if you attend. In some cases your entire grade is based on just two tests; in others there may be twenty components that determine your grade. Follow the grading system carefully so that you put your effort in the areas that count the most towards your grade.

Grading System: Grading will follow a standard 100 point scale, percentages, point system, or other rubric that corresponds to the final letter grade you will receive in the class. Note that percentages, points, etc., are basically all the same thing. Some colleges use a plus and minus system, others use letters only.

FINAL LETTER GRADE	PERCENTAGES	OR	FINAL LETTER GRADE	PERCENTAGES
A	93 to 100%		A	90 and above
A-	90 to 92%		B	80 to 89%
B+	87 to 89%		C	70 to 79%
B	83 to 86%		D	60 to 69%
B-	80 to 82%		F	below 59%
C+	77 to 79%			
C	73 to 76%			
C-	70 to 72%			
D	60 to 69%			
F	below 59%			

OR

FINAL LETTER GRADE	POINTS NEEDED
A	500
A-	475
B+	450
B	425
B-	400
C+	375
C	350
C-	325
D	300
F	<300

(Potential Categories—not exhaustive)

Tests: Midterm Exams (worth 20% each or 100 points)
Final Exam (worth 25% or 200 points)

Papers: Short to long (worth 10% or 50 points)
Research or informal

Projects: Multi-media shows
Service learning

Presentations: Short (five minutes) to long (thirty-five minutes)
Group or individual
Formal (power point) or informal (discussion of a topic in the news)

Homework: Collected and graded or not

Attendance: Not required or required (worth 10% or 100 points of grade)

Quizzes: Weekly
Announced or not

Term Outline: This will tell you what material is covered and when. It also provides dates when the tests are administered, when papers and any other assignments are due. Sometimes it will also tell if certain material is not covered and give specific information about special events that are relevant for the class.

The outline will typically be broken into days, parts, weeks or topics. Sometimes there will be specific information about what will be covered each class period during the semester (by day). In other situations the class material is just broken into large categories (by part). In between the two extremes course material is covered by week or topic, though the categories are not mutually exclusive.

Day 1:	Cover syllabus
Day 2:	Introduction to Anthropology
Day 3:	Indigenous populations of Brazil
Day 5:	Quiz
to Day 31:	Presentations

OR

Part 1:	Supply and Demand
Part 2:	Cost curves
Part 3:	Market structure

OR

Week 1:	Chapter 1
Week 2:	Chapters 2 and 3
Week 3:	First midterm exam

OR

Topic 1:	Management theories
Topic 2:	General environment
Topic 3:	…etc.
October __:	Midterm exam
Topic 6:	Decision making, etc.
December __:	Final exam

Make Friends in Class

If you have a friend in class, you will have somebody to get notes from if you miss. You can also compare notes to make sure neither of you missed anything. You will also have someone to study with and answer your questions. Perhaps more important is that you can answer their questions. If you can explain the class material to somebody else, then you know you have learned it well for yourself.

Take Effective, Detailed Notes

Listen carefully to the professor, and fill your iPad, laptop or notebook with this wisdom. In a lecture-based class, write down more than what you see on the power point slides, board or overheads. Elaborate with examples or jot down additional notes that will help you remember the material later. Don't necessarily copy everything word for word. Abbreviate, so that you can take notes faster. Many students make the mistake of thinking that all they need to do is write down and memorize whatever the professor has on the board.

> MAKE FRIENDS IN CLASS; TAKE EFFECTIVE, DETAILED NOTES; ASK QUESTIONS ABOUT ASSIGNMENTS EARLY; ASK QUESTIONS IN CLASS AND PARTICIPATE IN DISCUSSIONS.

MAKE SURE YOU UNDERSTAND WHAT YOU HAVE WRITTEN. If you copy notes in your own words, you are more likely to understand them. If you just repeat exactly what is on the board, you may struggle to interpret it later. Also, listen actively and attentively. Being in class and hearing the professor speak doesn't guarantee you are paying attention. You need to be engaged even if the class is entirely lecture. **GO BACK THROUGH YOUR NOTES AS SOON AS POSSIBLE AFTER CLASS** to fill in any information gaps.

PAY ATTENTION TO THE DETAILS, WHICH ARE OFTEN NOT WRITTEN DOWN. Some professors provide copies of their notes. Many professors get prepackaged power point slides with test banks and other materials. Often they will post them on Blackboard. Make sure to print them out and bring them to class. This does not mean you don't have to go to class, or that you don't have to take notes while in class. The notes provided are often just an outline. Crucial details are covered in class. As I said before, go to class.

Ask Questions About Assignments Early

At a job if you are given a task that you don't know how to do, you can try and figure it out on your own. It will take longer to accomplish, or you may do it incorrectly. This is also true with college assignments. You may have a paper, a research assignment or some other project that you don't understand completely. Don't spend hours on an assignment, if you are uncertain. Don't wait: go to the professor immediately and clarify the requirements.

Ask Questions in Class and Participate in Discussions

Don't be afraid to ask questions in class. Most professors view this as a sign you are interested and paying attention. Some of my best students have told me that asking questions, making comments or asking for clarification helps keep them engaged in the material. It can be hard to keep focused in a class, especially in classes lasting over an hour; asking an occasional question will help keep you focused. Participating in discussions also shows the professor you are interested and keeps you engaged.

> GET OFF TO A GOOD START; STUDY AT THE RIGHT TIME AND THE RIGHT PLACE; DO PRACTICE PROBLEMS FOR THE TESTS; GET THE BOOK AND READ THE BOOK; MAKE CONNECTIONS BETWEEN THE CLASS AND THE TEXTBOOK; USE AVAILABLE RESOURCES; KEEP AN OPEN MIND.

Be Polite

Approach class the same way you would a job. Don't let your cell phone ring and don't text during class. Don't get up in the middle of a class and walk out. If you need to leave work early, you tell your boss. If you need to leave class early, let the professor know.

Courtesy is especially important if you need to discuss your score on a test question or paper. Make sure you are right and have a valid argument. If you show you know the material, the professor will be more willing to consider your petition.

TIPS OUTSIDE OF CLASS AFTER THE SEMESTER BEGINS

Get Off to a Good Start

Create a schedule so you do not fall behind in your coursework. If you delay reading and studying for a week or two, you will pay the price by constantly having to catch up. Because classes often move fast, it can be difficult to keep up, let alone catch up. In addition, if you do poorly on an assignment early in the term, you will be unable to afford errors later.

Study at the Right Time in the Right Place

There is no shortage of distractions at college, so it is tempting to procrastinate. You will be busy with classes, extracurricular activities, a job, friends, etc. **SET ASIDE BLOCKS OF AN HOUR OR TWO A COUPLE TIMES EACH DAY WHERE YOUR JOB IS TO STUDY.**

For some students, studying in the dorms is easy. Other students need a quiet space away from everybody. There are desks hidden in the depths of the library and other areas that are very conducive to studying. Explore the campus and find the area that works best for you.

Find Old Tests

Many professors use questions from tests given in previous years. If possible find old tests from friends, roommates, or other students. Ask around. Even if the tests are different each semester, you will see the format of the test, the length and in general what is covered and how. Then you will know what to expect, about how difficult the test will be and how to prepare.

Do the Practice Problems for Tests

For classes in the sciences, math, accounting, statistics and other quantitative areas, you will be assigned practice questions from the textbook, study guide, website or some other source. The questions that are from the textbook or study guide are often identical to the test questions. If they are not identical, they are often the same question with just the numbers changed. Think of it as batting practice, a chance to prepare for the real thing. If you do the practice questions, you will be well prepared when you see the same or similar questions on the tests.

Get the Book

Get the book (electronic or paper) as soon as possible so you do not fall behind in the reading. SOMETIMES BOOK STORES RUN OUT, so don't wait a week or two into the semester. At a minimum, glance through the book. If you buy the book through the Internet or anywhere else other than the college book store, make sure you get the same book. There are many places that will sell you the textbook for less money, but in some cases it is a different edition or it is the international edition. These editions are often not the same as the one that your professor is using. The format of the book is different, so page numbers in one of the books do not correspond to page numbers in the other book. Different editions may include different chapters or material.

Do the Reading When it is Assigned

In high school you may have been able to get passable grades by studying the night before the test. This is nearly impossible in college. Do the reading immediately, and spend time studying, especially well before test time.

Make Connections Between the Class and the Textbook

In general, teachers cover the material in the book, but don't follow it exactly. They do not just lecture straight out of the book, and embellish on the material with their expertise. Make the connections between the book(s) and the information you get in class. AFTER CLASS, READ THE BOOK AND GO THROUGH YOUR NOTES AT THE SAME TIME. Rewrite your notes too, repetition helps your comprehension.

Professors read the books differently than you do. In some cases the professor may have written the book you are using in the class and will point out things they find most interesting. For most humanities classes the teacher likely has read the books multiple times (dozens or more) and will know nuances and the fine points that you will not. Sometimes a professor may just skim a book on a subject she has taught many times. In any situation the professor is going to view the book differently than you.

There are some topics professors think are very important that are only touched on by the book, and so they will cover them more in depth. There are other items they feel are unnecessary, and so may skip them entirely. Some professors put material straight from the book that was not covered in class on their tests. **In general, the topics that are emphasized both in class and in the book are those that are most likely to be on tests.**

Use Available Resources

Use the resources that professors provide. Most colleges have access to technology, such as Blackboard, where professors will post syllabi, old tests and sometimes answer some of your questions directly.

There are **many other resources available also, such as tutoring facilities, writing centers, and language labs-use them.** Most students find certain classes such as Chemistry and Calculus more difficult than other classes. There are typically scheduled hours at tutoring or learning centers where you can go for help. Conversely, if there are tutors available for a class this means that many students have had trouble with the class in the past and you will likely find it difficult; be prepared.

Support is there, you just need to find it. Some students say that there is very little support available to them in order for them to succeed academically; others say there is a lot. Both are correct. There is a lot of support available; you just need to find it. **Ask your professors or other students.**

Keep an Open Mind

Professors have different styles and personalities in the classroom. Some think their job is just to impart their expertise through lectures. Others think they have to entertain you with stories, jokes and films. Some professors will nurture you, guiding you along each step, while others think it is time for you do all things by yourself and will not provide any guidance. Most have something to offer; try to find out what it is. Don't stereotype or make generalizations about professors based on their gender, race or any other characteristic.

If You Have an Incompetent Professor Let Somebody Know

It is rare, but it is possible that you may get an incompetent professor. Not somebody who is hard, not somebody who is disorganized, not somebody who is boring or has some other characteristic that you do not like, but somebody who honestly does not know what they are doing. If it is just an annoyance, do your best and avoid that person in the future. If it is a serious problem, go see the department chair.

PAPER-WRITING TIPS

When a paper is assigned, the professor will usually describe the requirements in great detail. **MAKE SURE YOU FOLLOW INSTRUCTIONS EXACTLY.** Professors vary in their expectations on papers; some take off a lot of points for spelling and grammar, others do not; some require specific formatting, while others do not. If you are assigned a research paper, be sure to follow the guidelines for sources and references.

Remember your audience. You use informal language and grammar when talking with friends, texting, and using social media. As you know from high school, formal communication is necessary with employers and professors. Don't use slang, abbreviations or other informal methods of communicating in your papers. **MAKE SURE YOUR PAPERS USE FORMAL LANGUAGE AND GRAMMAR.** Most schools have a writing center that can help you with your papers.

SPEND EXTRA TIME ON THE BEGINNING OF YOUR PAPER. The first page sets the tone for the rest of your paper. If you start it well, the professor is more likely to expect the rest of the paper to be good and give you the benefit of the doubt when grading your paper. Write at least two drafts (preferably more) of your paper. Write the first draft as soon as you can. Then go back to it and re-write it later. If possible, have a classmate proofread your paper for any mistakes or clarifications that may be needed.

TEST-TAKING TIPS

You heard it in high school, but it is worth repeating: **READ THE TEST DIRECTIONS CAREFULLY! MAKE SURE YOU ANSWER THE QUESTION BEING ASKED.** If a question asks you to write about two of three topics, be sure you write about two. If you are asked to answer four of six questions, don't be that student who answers three, or six. When given an essay question, be sure to use formal language and grammar. If asked list the most important topics, then bullet points may be used.

In some situations, including tests, you may know exactly what the teacher is looking for and know exactly how to answer the question. Sometimes you may know the material but be unable to show the teacher that you do. **IF A TEST QUESTION IS CONFUSING, ASK FOR CLARIFICATION.** Make sure you do it in a manner that shows you know the material. Ask the question, "I think the answer to this is _____ because of such and such reason." Asking in this manner shows that you know the material, and the professor may point you down the right path.

Don't be confrontational. If you say something such as: "Your questions are confusing." "We didn't cover this in class." "This isn't a fair question." you will put the professor on the defensive, and you may not receive the help you want. This type of question tells the professor you don't know the material.

TIPS WITH PROFESSORS

I have met some college dropouts who are sure the reason they flunked out of college is because the professors were out to get them. There may be a professor somewhere who is vindictive and flunks students out of spite. This is an aberration. **STUDENTS DON'T FAIL CLASSES BECAUSE PROFESSORS WANT THEM TO FAIL. STUDENTS FAIL CLASSES BECAUSE THEY DO NOT MEET THE COURSE REQUIREMENTS OR THE PROFESSOR'S EXPECTATIONS.**

There are a variety of methods to find information about the quality of professors. **GO TO THE POTENTIAL TEACHER'S WEBSITE IF THEY HAVE ONE.** Most colleges have students complete evaluation forms about the class at the end of the semester. For public colleges, the evaluations are public domain. You can see summaries of past student evaluations on professors and their courses. Sometimes this information is housed in the library or some other public space.

Evaluations can range from very helpful to completely useless. In some cases the professors pick the questions that are on the evaluation form. In other cases there are so few questions that they do not provide data whether the professor showed up on time and covered any material. In some cases bad professors get good ratings only because they hand out a large number of undeserved As. **USE THE TEACHER EVALUATIONS, BUT REALIZE THEY MAY NOT TELL THE ENTIRE STORY.**

There are also websites such as myprofessorsucks.com, where students anonymously post rankings and comments about professors they have had. It is no surprise that the postings are mainly from students who feel strongly because they failed a class or otherwise had problems. Other students may post something on these websites because they got an easy A in the class. While it can be entertaining to read these evaluations, usually there is not much to be learned from them.

> STUDENTS DON'T FAIL CLASSES BECAUSE PROFESSORS WANT THEM TO FAIL. THEY FAIL CLASSES BECAUSE THEY DO NOT MEET THE COURSE REQUIREMENTS OR THE PROFESSOR'S EXPECTATIONS.

Get to know your professors a little. Ask them a question after class or stop by during their office hours. Most professors want to get to know you, but you may have to make the effort. If you are taking a full class load, you may have five professors. If a teacher has four classes with 45 students each, they have to get to know close to 200 people over a course of a few months. Semester after semester, year after year.

At the end of a semester some professors look for reasons to bump up your grade. If they add up your test scores, papers and other assignments and see an 88.5 average, they ask themselves some questions. Do I know who this student is? If they know you, they are more likely to round the B+ up to an A-. It is easy to get lost in the masses of 100 or more students. You can make it easy for them to give you the benefit of the doubt by getting to know them.

Different teachers have different objectives for their students. I find that students today tend to be smart, but do not pay much attention to the broader world. One of my goals as a professor is to expose students to current events within the context of the material. I always enjoy when a student comes up after class and says I heard the news about such and such topic that is related to the class. It shows they are paying attention and applying what they have learned.

The How-To-Take-This-Test guides assume that all professors teach, give tests, and evaluate students in the same way. Some will just give only multiple-choice questions; others will give all essay questions. Some teachers think working in groups is important. Other teachers think in-class participation is important. The key is to recognize how a professor approaches their class so that you can spend your time studying wisely. **Professors want you to succeed in their class; each one has a different way for you show it.**

Use Office Hours and Ask for Help When Needed

If you are struggling with a class, get help as soon as possible. Don't wait until the end of the semester. By then, it is much too late. If you have problems with class material, go see the teacher directly. Yes, it is easier to ask a question with email, especially if it is something about a bad test grade, but a professor may be better able to fully answer your questions in person. Again, showing up in person lets the professor know you care about the class.

> Get to know your professors. Ask them a question after class or stop by during their office hours. Most professors want to get to know you, but you may have to make the effort.

When I get an email from a student saying, "I did poorly on the test and I want to know what to do," I always tell them to stop by my office, because I cannot help them with that generic statement. If I see them in person, with their test and notes, I can see where potential problems likely came from and provide tailored advice for them.

When asking questions about a past test, an upcoming project, paper, homework or any other assignment, be prepared. **Ask specific questions about the material.** "How do I find the integral of this problem? I made it to this point and don't know how to get to the next step." Don't use generalities, such as—can you explain integrals to me, or I don't understand statistics.

When a student comes by my office and it is clear that they have read the book, looked through their notes and have completed all the required work, I always go beyond what is necessary to make sure they learn what they need to know. If a student comes by my office one hour before a test and asks, "Do I need to know this?" it is clear that they did not do the required work. Professors don't like to see students unprepared. It shows that they do not care about the material, the class or the professor. If a student does not care about the class, it is very likely that the professor will not care the student.

If you are going to ask questions about anything other than topics related to the class, make sure you word them appropriately. Ask something like, "Where should I put my energy?" not, "What do I need to know for the test?"

Show That You Work Hard, Don't Say That You Do

Something every professor has heard way too many times is, "but I worked so hard." We know who works hard and who doesn't. The student updating their Facebook page or shopping in class is not working hard. (Yes, we know you're doing it!) The student who shows up to every class, asks questions, and participates in discussions likely works hard. The student who stops by office hours with good questions works hard. The student who sleeps through class or who misses half the classes isn't working hard.

A student's perception of working hard is likely different from the professor's. A student may think that studying for five hours the night before a test is a lot. A professor thinks that they should have been studying ten hours a week for the past month.

Keep in mind, many professors want to give good grades. I personally much prefer grading A work (on tests, projects, and papers) than any other work because it is easier for me. When I read an A paper, it is well written, follows the required format and explains the topic well. When I grade an A test, my questions are answered completely and it shows that the student understands the material. I am happy with A work and so is the student.

It takes much more time to distinguish between other grades. Do I take four points off for this question or five? Is this a D paper or can I justify giving it a C-? It takes more time and more effort to weed through variations of different grade levels. **SHOW US YOU ARE WORKING HARD AND DESERVE AN A; WE'LL GIVE IT TO YOU.**

Show Maturity

I once handed back a test with a failing grade to one student. He came up after class and we talked about it. He said, "I guess I should have studied more than three hours for this test." I said yes that would make a big difference. A little later he stopped by my office hours with good questions, showing he was working more, his test scores improved and he did well in the class. It was clear he recognized the need to work more and he did.

Use Technology Appropriately

In general use email and other technologies as directed by the professor. Many professors will encourage you to contact them via email, but some still do not like to use this form of communication. In many situations it is difficult to answer questions thoroughly through email, particularly difficult questions about class material.

IF YOU USE EMAIL TO ASK QUESTIONS, KEEP THE MESSAGE SHORT. Professors are busy; they may not read a long email. Also make sure that you identify yourself, "Hi, this is so-and-so from your such-and-such class." We will not know who mrpoker57@… is. In your email be polite, succinct, and professional.

Professors are increasingly using Blackboard and other types of educational technology. Professors use such programs to hold discussions and may ask students to use them to turn in work or answer questions. Programs like Blackboard can be used for quizzes and students can monitor their class grades on it. Be sure you know how much (or little) it is used in each class and use it accordingly.

If You Need Special Accommodations Let the Professor Know In Person as Soon as Possible

Some students have a learning disability or other impairment that impacts their ability to take notes or tests or otherwise makes academic work more difficult. Professors are usually understanding and if you have registered with the appropriate student support service center, they received notification about your status. It helps though if you introduce yourself and talk to them about it personally, even if it is for just a minute.

Be Proactive

If you are going to miss a test because of a previous engagement, let the teacher know as soon as possible. If you have three finals on the same day, you may be able to get one moved to another day. **TAKE CARE OF ANYTHING THAT WILL INTERFERE WITH YOUR CLASS AS SOON AS YOU KNOW ABOUT IT.**

Make Strong Connections with a Couple of Professors

I had a student stop by my office and ask for a recommendation for an internship. I sort of recognized her and asked which of my classes she was in. When I looked it up, I saw she had one of the better averages and had received an A in my class. I did not remember her well because she hid in the back of the class, never participated and did not do anything to differentiate herself.

SHOW MATURITY; USE TECHNOLOGY APPROPRIATELY; IF YOU NEED SPECIAL ACCOMMODATIONS, LET THE PROFESSOR KNOW IN PERSON AS SOON AS POSSIBLE; BE PROACTIVE; AND MAKE STRONG CONNECTIONS WITH A FEW OF YOUR PROFESSORS.

I wrote a very generic letter saying that she did OK in my class. For students I know, I tailor their letter of recommendation to the internship they are seeking, which I am sure makes the organization much more likely to hire them.

YOU WILL LIKELY NEED A FEW LETTERS OF RECOMMENDATION FOR A JOB, LAW SCHOOL OR SOME OTHER FUTURE ENDEAVOR. In addition to making sure the professor likes you, be sure to pick a professor who knows you well. **MAKE SURE AT LEAST A COUPLE PROFESSORS KNOW YOU WELL AND WILL BE AVAILABLE TO HELP YOU IN THE FUTURE.**

IF POSSIBLE, WORK INDEPENDENTLY WITH A PROFESSOR. One of the best ways to make connections with a professor is to work with them on an independent study class, a research project or some other method where it is just the two of you working together. Colleges are increasing the number of opportunities for students to engage in research, conduct case studies, participate in service learning activities and other projects that require lots of interaction between students and professors.

Some professors will say in class that they are available to work with you on a project related to their class. Other professors may tell you that a particular paper or project you completed was very good and that you can turn it in to a larger research project. If a professor does not approach you, ask them. This is a great way to explore an area of interest and set yourself apart from other college graduates when you finish.

TIPS BEYOND THE CLASSROOM

There are some things you can do specifically related to classes that will help with academics. There are also activities not directly related to classes that can help boost your grades.

Be Aware that Some Students Don't Care About College

Some students attend college because their parents want them to, they don't know what else to do or are just doing what their friends do. Many of these students get by for a semester or two before flunking out. Others just barely get through a year or two then drop out. You should be able to tell if someone does not enjoy college. These people will drag you down. **SPEND YOUR VALUABLE TIME ONLY WITH STUDENTS WHO ENJOY COLLEGE AND WANT TO BE THERE.**

Find Smart Friends

It has been well documented that the people around a person impact their behavior, either positively or negatively (the peer effect). It is no surprise that peers in college can have large impacts on a student's behavior. If you have friends who do well in college, they can push you to excel or help you out if you are struggling. In addition, you can see what they are doing to succeed and follow their lead. In some cases there may be a friendly competition to see who can get better grades.

Find a Job on Campus

If you work, find a job on campus where you learn more about the school. In addition, you have an opportunity to make friends outside your traditional circle. You may get a chance to interact with professors and see them in a way that is not possible in class. If you work on campus you are more a part of the community, if you are part of the community you are more likely to feel that you are a part of the college, and if you feel you are a part of the college you will work harder at completing your degree.

Use ALL Available Resources

There are likely dozens of centers and groups with many people available to help you in just about every way you may need. Use the career development center. Be sure to get advising either through a professor or from the advising center. Go to the financial aid office to see if you qualify. There are also student groups that can help provide support for students from diverse backgrounds and with a variety of needs.

Seek Support From as Many Sources as Possible

There are both official and unofficial channels to help you navigate college. Official sources of support include your advisor and RA. Department secretaries and program assistants often know more about how the college system works than anybody else. They can help you get into closed classes, guide you towards the better teachers and tell you how to find assistance if you are having problems.

Have Fun

Try everything, especially if it's something new. Go to the foreign film festival, attend Cinco de Mayo, and participate in intramural sports. There are so many activities, get involved and have fun. If you are enjoying yourself while in college, you are more likely to stay and finish.

Take Advantage of the Opportunities

Look around: you will find that there are internships, study abroad opportunities, and clubs for hundreds of interests. You might even be able to get paid for some of these activities. Many colleges have money for students to conduct research, study abroad, talk to incoming students, and do other activities that are fun and are resume builders.

Pay Attention to Your Mental and Physical Health

It is easy to get so caught up in studying, hanging out with friends, and other activities that you don't do things that recharge your battery. Be sure to make time for exercising, church, or any other activity that helps revitalize you. Ignoring your physical and mental health will only be detrimental to your college experience.

REMEMBER...

Colleges/universities want you to succeed!

Be prepared for difficult courses; take the tough courses from a supportive professor.

Attend class; be on time; read the class syllabus carefully; focus on the assignments that have the greatest impact on your grade.

Set aside blocks of an hour or two a couple times each day where your job is to study.

Use the many resources available, such as tutoring facilities, writing centers, and language labs.

Read test directions carefully! Make sure you answer the questions being asked; if a test question is confusing, ask for clarification.

If you are struggling with a class, get help as soon as possible.

Show professors you are working hard and deserve an A; they'll give it to you!

Spend your valuable time only with students who enjoy college and want to be there.

chapter 8
POTENTIAL PROBLEMS

We all encounter setbacks and problems. Some of us respond by retreating, going back to something familiar. Others view these as bumps in the road, something temporary that they confront, navigate and then continue on with life. Most of us ignore some problems, work through others in a less than satisfactory way, and manage to overcome other tribulations. The ability to persevere and conquer problems is paramount to success in life.

College can be a great experience, but it can also be difficult and trying at times. Difficulty generally arises from two broad areas. The first is struggling with academics. The second is non-academic areas. These can involve depression, difficult roommates, finances, and even crime. These issues can negatively impact college performance. Some students are more at risk of dropping out of college, such as minorities, first generation students, students whose parents are divorced and students from lower socio-economic backgrounds.

Students who flunk out are those who are dismissed from college because their grades drop below the required 2.0 minimum for a certain period of time, so that the college cannot justify letting them continue to enroll. Students who drop out are those who leave permanently before they graduate, even though their grades are adequate. Sometimes the two are related; when students are doing poorly and decide to drop out instead of making an attempt to improve their grades and stay in college.

Remember that professors view classes differently from you. The teacher may not see that you are struggling. Females are more likely to ask for help than males, which is one of the reasons females are more likely to graduate. **FOR ANY LEGITIMATE PROBLEM, GO SEE THE PROFESSOR. DO IT AS EARLY AS POSSIBLE, NOT AT THE END OF THE SEMESTER WHEN IT IS TOO LATE TO FIX.**

There are also many minor problems students may encounter. Colleges have different departments responsible for different areas. For example if you have a problem with your transcript, go to the registrar's office; if you have a problem with your roommate, go to the residence life office. Use the website; ask staff, professors or other students to find where to go for the particular issue. This chapter will describe the main problems students face and provide tips on how to deal with them.

ACADEMIC PROBLEMS

Problem:
YOU PROCRASTINATED

SHORT RUN: DO AS MUCH AS YOU CAN. It is better to turn in a paper that gets a D (60%) instead of not turning in anything and getting a zero. For a test, study as much as you can, then show up and take it. Do not miss a test. You can still salvage a passing grade in a class if you get a 50 percent on the first test; you can't if you get a 20. Drink coffee, chug an energy drink, stay up late. Do whatever you can. Simple math shows that averaging a 65 in your final grade instead of a 0 gives you a chance at a C or better, instead of a D or an F.

Procrastination is something we do to set ourselves up for failure. As soon as you can, **FIND OUT WHY YOU PROCRASTINATE.** Is it a lack of interest, effort, anxiety, or the inability to focus? Are you afraid of failure or success? Are you a perfectionist? Procrastination is extremely common, and there are dozens of reasons we do it.

If it is the end of the semester and you have multiple tests and papers coming up, make sure you **PRIORITIZE.** If there is a class you are going to fail no matter what, don't do anything more for that class. Put all your time into classes that you can still pass. **MAKE SURE YOU PUT THE MOST TIME INTO PROJECTS THAT HAVE THE HIGHEST PAYOFF.** Spend your time studying or working on something that is a large part of your grade, not something that that does not count much. **SAY NO TO ANYTHING THAT TAKES TIME AWAY FROM YOUR COURSEWORK.**

Problem:
YOU PERFORMED POORLY ON A TEST OR PAPER

TIMING IS EVERYTHING. I always have students email me at the end of each semester after final grades have been posted and ask, "I failed your class. Is there anything I can do to change my grade?" The answer is always **no.** The term is over, and grades are finalized with the Registrar.

Some students come by my office immediately after doing poorly on the first quiz or test and say, "I didn't do well on the first test, is there anything I can do?" The answer is always **YES.**

College professors want to help you, but we don't pass students who haven't bothered to do any work all semester or come to our office hours. **IF YOU ARE DOING POORLY, GO FOR HELP IMMEDIATELY.** Teachers appreciate students who learn from their mistakes. We love to see students work hard and turn a D into a B.

Problem:
YOU RECEIVED NOTICE THAT YOU ARE FAILING A CLASS

Colleges notify students if their grades are unsatisfactory midway through the semester. Professors send a list of students doing poorly to the registrar's office so that they can notify failing students. Go to the professor as soon as you are notified and talk to them about improving your grade. Everyone wants to help the person who wants to help him/herself.

PAY ATTENTION TO DEADLINES. Up to a certain point in the semester, you can drop a class without it appearing on your transcript. You may be able to add a class that only meets in the second half of the term. You may also be able to get refunds for full or partial tuition when you drop a class, up to a certain date. Be careful about dropping classes though. Be aware of how many credit hours you need for full-time status. If you fall to part-time status, you may lose financial aid.

Problem:
YOU DON'T SEE THE RELEVANCE OF A CLASS OR IT IS BORING

Sometimes students don't do their best in classes because they don't see the relevance of the topic or how it fits into their career goals. Just as a basketball player doesn't only shoot a basketball all the time; they lift weights, they run sprints, and do other things not directly related to their job. They are training their bodies so that they are prepared. Sometimes it is the same thing in college; the exposure to a variety of topics and methods expands your mind and will help you solve future job and life problems.

Problem:
YOU ARE ON ACADEMIC PROBATION

Students are put on academic probation if they fail to maintain a minimum of a C average (2.0 on a 4.0 point scale). You will receive a warning that you are on academic probation, so you have a little time to change the situation, before being asked to leave college. Meet with your advisor and your professors immediately to see how you can improve. Take the warning to heart and change what you are doing immediately.

Problem:
YOU ARE OVERWHELMED

This is not uncommon. Today's college students have not just their school work but lots of other non-academic activities to keep them busy all the time. **BREAK TASKS AND PROJECTS DOWN INTO SMALLER PIECES. THEN PRIORITIZE THEM.** Remember college is your primary responsibility, so your school work comes first. You will spend much more time and money getting your degree, if you fail a class. Put other activities on hold, and make time to pass the class. Set aside a certain number of hours each day to study, read, write and do all the necessary work for your classes.

Problem:
YOU HATE THE CLASSES IN YOUR MAJOR

Actually, this is good news. Congratulations on discovering this sooner rather than later. **IF YOU DO NOT LIKE THE CLASSES IN YOUR MAJOR, CHANGE IT.** You may have started your major because it was recommended to you by a parent or high school guidance counselor. You have to do what is best for you.

Problem:
YOU THINK YOU MAY HAVE PICKED THE WRONG MAJOR

It's not uncommon to feel unsure about your major. If you haven't already, take time away from classes in your major to fulfill other college requirements. One of the great things about college is exploring a variety of subjects. One of these courses may resonate with you, and you may discover a new major this way. In addition, you may be asking yourself, "What if I don't like the job my major is preparing me for?" Picking a major does not force you into a job you don't like for the rest of your life. Few of us get the perfect job right after college.

Problem:
YOU HAVE A LEARNING DISABILITY

You may have a diagnosed disability such as Attention Deficit Hyperactivity Disorder (ADHD) that causes problems or you may have a learning disability that is not diagnosed. **GO TO THE STUDENT SUPPORT SERVICE CENTER**. They will help make arrangements for you for taking tests and other areas that you are struggling with.

WHAT NOT TO DO WHEN YOU ARE STRUGGLING

When you face challenges in college, sometimes what you don't do is just as important as what you do. Avoid these common mistakes that many students make.

Don't Make Excuses

Every professor could write a book about the excuses they have heard for why a student did not do well on a test or in a class: My mom's sick, my pet died, my grandma fell down the stairs, my car broke down, the computer crashed, the printer doesn't work, my backpack was stolen, and on and on. You are expected to be a mature, responsible, independent adult. If there is a legitimate reason why you can't get something done, go see the professor immediately, **BEFORE** it's due, and work it out.

Don't Overload Yourself

If you do poorly one semester, don't try to make up for it the next term by taking extra classes. Perhaps you failed two of the five classes you took. You may think you need to take seven classes to correct this (five plus the two) to get back on track to graduate. It is likely you will just be even more overwhelmed. Talk to your advisor, and make gradual changes to fix your academic record. If needed, take a class or two over the summer to catch up.

Don't Ask For Preferential Treatment

Don't go up to the professor in class on the day of the test and say, "I'm not ready. Can I take the test later?" Don't ask for an extension on a paper the day it's due. Unless you've been in the hospital getting a kidney transplant and have a surgeon's note, you've just put the professor in a very awkward situation. There are no legitimate reasons—short of an emergency room visit, for which you have proof—that would entice a teacher to give you a privilege the rest of the class isn't getting.

> DON'T MAKE EXCUSES; DON'T OVERLOAD YOURSELF; DON'T ASK FOR PREFERENTIAL TREATMENT; DON'T GUILT A PROFESSOR...
>
> **DON'T CHEAT!**

Don't Cheat

Tempting as it may be to buy a paper off the internet, turn in other people's work, cheat on tests, or otherwise cut corners, **DON'T**. Serious consequences will follow. Cheating appears on your college record, which in turn will decrease your chances of transferring to another school or getting into graduate school and may negatively influence future employers. It may even get you kicked out of college.

Don't Guilt a Professor

At the end of every semester a few students always email me or talk to me about their less than satisfactory grades. After some realize that there is no way for them to improve their grade, they try other tactics. They will argue, "if I don't give them a good grade, then I'll lose my financial aid," or "now I won't get into law school and my parents will kill me." This is, of course, unfortunate, but grades are based on a student's class performance. I feel bad for them but, I do not base my grades on anything other than a student's performance in my class.

REMEMBER YOUR COLLEGE WANTS YOU TO GRADUATE! NO MATTER WHAT YOUR PROBLEM IS, FIND HELP. There are people on campus whose job is to make sure students succeed. Find them and use their expertise. It is hard for most of us to admit to ourselves and others that we need help, but all of us do from time to time. **IN SOME SITUATIONS DOING LITTLE THINGS CAN MAKE A BIG DIFFERENCE. IN OTHER CASES, THERE MAY NOT BE AN EASY SOLUTION, BUT THERE IS A SOLUTION.**

> REMEMBER, YOUR COLLEGE WANTS YOU TO GRADUATE! NO MATTER WHAT YOUR PROBLEM, FIND HELP!
>
> HELP IS ALWAYS AVAILABLE.

NON-ACADEMIC PROBLEMS

Nearly every college student will hit a rough patch at some point. Issues will range from small to enormous. Some students confront demons they did not have previously. The next part of the chapter examines some of the internal and external issues that college students may face and methods of coping with them.

I believe that the largest factor influencing most student's decision to drop out of college is not the inability to do the work required but because of other issues. In over two decades of teaching, every semester, I have witnessed at least one student experience, sometimes many, a legitimate problem that causes them to drop out, such as parents getting divorced or a friend from home dying in a car accident.

Students may encounter a personal problem, such as a relationship breakup, an illness like mono, or a bout with depression. And sometimes the problem is just growing up and the student coming to grips with being an adult.

Many surveys have shown that well over half of college students felt hopeless at some point, almost half were depressed to the point that they had trouble functioning, a huge majority were overwhelmed, and some even considered suicide. That's the bad news; **THE GOOD NEWS IS THAT HELP IS AVAILABLE.** Treatment exists for depression, eating disorders, anxiety, insomnia and almost any other mental or physical problem you may experience.

If a problem occurs, ask yourself whether the issue is so severe that you can't stay in school. If you will be unable to give your best and pass your courses with satisfactory grades, then make taking care of your problem a priority. **ADDRESS ANY SERIOUS PROBLEM IMMEDIATELY WITH YOUR ADVISOR, YOUR PROFESSORS, AND POSSIBLY THE ADMINISTRATION.**

Everyone has problems—sometimes small, sometimes major. There is no doubt that one of the hardest things to handle as you go through your adult life is to continue with your work, school and family as you or people you know and love have difficulties. Every college professor has heard, "I have not been in class for the past month because my grandfather is sick." Despite compassion for the student, professors just can't give out sympathy grades. Regardless of personal life, students are still responsible for getting the work done or for working with the administration to obtain a withdrawal for the course. **IN ANY SITUATION THERE ARE PEOPLE AVAILABLE FOR YOU TO TALK TO AND IN SOME CASES THERE ARE PEOPLE THERE SPECIFICALLY TO HELP YOU WITH PARTICULAR PROBLEMS.** This includes the staff at the health center, the Student Affairs office, residence life and many others.

Physical Health Problems

If you are a typical college student at some point you will likely eat poorly, sleep erratically, stay awake all night studying, party too late or otherwise not take good care of yourself. Not to mention that you will be around other sick students and be stressed out from time to time. You will likely get sick; the key is **TO TAKE CARE OF ANY ILLNESS IMMEDIATELY.** Go to the **STUDENT HEALTH SERVICES OFFICE AND HAVE THE NURSES CHECK YOU OUT. THIS ALSO PROVIDES A PAPER DOCUMENT IF YOU NEED AN EXCUSE FOR WHY YOU MISSED CLASS.**

It does not matter if it is pink eye, mono, a broken leg, or the flu, **LET YOUR PROFESSORS KNOW AS SOON AS YOU CAN—THIS IS A GOOD OCCASION TO USE EMAIL.** If you have any special physical needs, require special medication, have hearing or sight problems, or need certain accommodations, take care of it immediately.

Psychological Health Problems

The number of students reporting some kind of psychological problem has increased greatly over the past few decades. College has become more stressful. There is also more awareness and fewer stigmas associated with having a psychological health problem. **AS A RESULT, ALMOST ALL COLLEGES PROVIDE COUNSELING SERVICES.** The health service center has social workers or psychologists who can talk to you about any type of issue. These services are usually free for students.

Many people find it difficult to ask for help. **IF YOU FACE A PSYCHOLOGICAL HEALTH PROBLEM, GET IT ADDRESSED IMMEDIATELY.** It may be one of the hardest things you will ever do, but do it. Many people think that it is a sign of weakness to admit a problem, it is just the opposite. It shows strength and maturity to admit when we need help and to go out and get it.

Depression

Depression can be one of the most debilitating conditions a person can face. Whether it is mild or severe, depression impedes success in college. There are some simple things you can do: find a doctor or somebody to talk to. Do things for yourself, photography or whatever you enjoy; write things down. Try to exercise and eat well. Life can be hard, but it is not the end of the world; think about the simple pleasures like a hot shower. It is so hard to remember when you are depressed, but things work out, not always perfectly, but they do.

Stress

There has probably never been a student who has not experienced stress at some point. Don't worry about doing everything perfectly. Make a list; prioritize what needs to be completed and what can wait. **DON'T BE TOO HARD ON YOURSELF. TAKE TIME FOR YOURSELF**—exercise, play video games, do whatever you like. In the grand scheme of things, compared to many other parts of life, in college the stakes are pretty low. Often when it comes to coursework, the absolute worst thing that can happen is that you fail a test or a class. The class can be repeated. Try to keep things in perspective. Whatever is stressing you out may not be as big a deal as you think.

Anxiety

After stress, worrying is probably the next biggest issue facing most college students. In addition to worrying about things specifically related to college, you may be worried about finding a job you like, or one that pays well, or something else about the future. Don't worry too much about what your degree is, there is always graduate school, certificates or some other post-college education that you can use to fill in any area you may lack. In addition, many employers will pay for MBAs and other graduate degrees.

Isolation

In high school maybe you couldn't wait to get away, but now that you are away you may feel lonely. Being homesick is natural. Your campus may be large and overwhelming. Adjusting to college can be a difficult process because you may not feel connected to anything at first. Colleges have many activities, which are a great way to meet other people. **SIGN UP FOR SOMETHING THAT INTERESTS YOU.**

Alienation

Certain populations are underrepresented or marginalized by parts of society. The good news is that colleges are much more accepting of differences in people than practically any other type of institution. It may take a little time but if you try you will find support networks, clubs, friends and other people you feel comfortable with.

Harassment and Assault

If you are harassed by another student, a teaching assistant, professor, or anybody else report it immediately to an academic advisor, resident assistant or somebody else. Bullying from other students happens less in college than in high school, but it does occur. Colleges are usually very safe, however if something happens report it to campus security, the residence advisor and police immediately if it is a serious crime.

Drugs and Alcohol

I am not condoning this, but let's be honest, experimentation with different types of drugs and drinking is a common occurrence on most college campuses. Any type of substance can impair not only school work but relationships and other areas of your life. **HAVE FUN, BUT BE CAREFUL.**

Gambling, Video Games, and Other Potentially Addictive Activities

Poker, Madden Football and other leisure activities are a great way to have fun and reduce stress-in moderation. You may find yourself spending dozens of hours a week on gambling or video games. It may be a form of procrastination or you may have an addictive personality. Either way it is taking time away from studying, working and socializing. If it is an addiction, seek help; the sooner you do the easier it is overcome.

Problems with Family or Peers

There are many ways relationships with other people can cause problems. Problems with family stem from a variety of sources. On one end there may be little or no encouragement from your family. On the other extreme your parents may be overly involved in your life.

If you are a first generation college student, your parents likely don't understand what you are going through. You may not get emotional support from your parents. This makes it harder, but ultimately your college degree is for you, not anybody else.

Most parents today are more involved with their children than with previous generations. This is a great thing unless parents get over involved and do everything for their kids. These 'helicopter' parents have trouble letting their kids make their own decisions, including picking colleges, choosing classes and deciding on a major. **COLLEGE IS THE BEST TIME TO START DOING THINGS FOR YOURSELF**—and making your own decisions.

Another potential problem is parental pressure. Your family likely wants what is best for you, but their well-intentioned advice about classes, majors, jobs, and careers can be stressful. The best thing to do is to be honest with your family and tell them what you want to do. This is not to say that you should not listen to your parents.

Your parents may try to make you feel guilty. They may compare you to your stellar older brother or younger sister. Though you may feel obligated to do what your parents want, if you spend your life doing something somebody else wants, you will be miserable. You have to be happy with what you are doing.

In addition to pressure from family, you may be pressured by a partner or friends into doing things you don't want to do. Learn to be yourself-be true to what you want and who you are.

You will change while you are in college. College should be a time of enormous personal growth, and most family and friends will applaud this. But some people may be threatened by your growth or jealous of it. Relationships with people you have been close to may change or even disappear.

Money

The cost of college is a realistic, external money problem. Beyond that, most of your money problems during college are self-imposed. Are you living beyond your means? Are you working to buy fancy clothes and expensive meals, living pay check to pay check? Are you piling up credit card debt on items you could probably live without until you finish school? Remember, long term wages go up with a college degree, so being a poor college student is just a temporary situation.

Other Problems

There are problems beyond what I've listed here. If you are not enjoying yourself, are not growing emotionally and intellectually, and do not like your classes or major, take a step back. Make sure you are a good fit for that school. There are other options. It is not just attend this college or don't attend college at all. Transferring is a possibility if you are not happy with your present experience.

If you hate college, don't do it. Ask yourself, why do I want to be in college? Does it provide an opportunity to improve yourself? Does it open doors for a future career? Maybe college is not for you at age 18, but maybe it will be for you when you are 20. Maybe college is not for you at all. Don't attend college because you think you have to.

Are you going to college just to get credentials? Are you going to college because your parents want you to? Are you going to college because you feel it is expected of you? Make sure you are there for the right reasons. **SOMETIMES**

THE PROBLEM IS NOT COLLEGE, IT IS SOMETHING ELSE, SO DON'T CON-FUSE PROBLEMS STEMMING FROM COLLEGE (STRESS WRITING PAPERS) TO OTHER PROBLEMS (PERSONAL, RELATIONSHIPS, ETC.).

In the long run, college is the right choice for many people. You will hit some problems in life; dealing with them in college will help you learn how to navigate them later in life. The next chapter will provide a few of the many reasons why you should attend college and stick with it until graduation.

REMEMBER...

FOR LEGITIMATE PROBLEMS, GO SEE THE PROFESSOR.
DO IT AS EARLY AS POSSIBLE, NOT AT THE END OF THE
SEMESTER WHEN IT IS TOO LATE TO FIX.

MAKE SURE YOU PUT THE MOST TIME INTO PROJECTS
THAT HAVE THE HIGHEST PAYOFF.

PAY ATTENTION TO DEADLINES.

BREAK TASKS AND PROJECTS DOWN INTO SMALLER
PIECES. THEN PRIORITIZE THEM.

IF YOU DO NOT LIKE THE CLASSES IN YOUR MAJOR,
CHANGE IT.

REMEMBER, COLLEGES WANT YOU TO GRADUATE!
NO MATTER WHAT YOUR PROBLEM IS, FIND HELP.

DON'T BE TOO HARD ON YOURSELF.

HAVE FUN, BUT BE CAREFUL!

chapter 9

REASONS TO ATTEND AND FINISH COLLEGE

There are many points when young adults can get side tracked or discouraged about the college process. Some people feel overwhelmed by the application process itself, others are unsure about what they want to do with their lives and decide to not attend college at all. Other students may start college but drop out in their first year because they don't like their major, are lonely or experience some other problem. Still others may spend a year or two in college, drop out with the intention of eventually returning and graduating, but never do.

Most people want a full and satisfying life. For the majority of us this includes having a sense of worth, an identity of who we are and figuring out our place in the world. Part of this comes from what we do on a regular basis, so is typically tied to our jobs and career. Work is a source of not only money but also one's identity. Sometimes directly, sometimes indirectly, college helps us discover what we want to do with our lives, thus helps us with our sense of identity, of who we are and what makes us special.

Reasons to Attend College

Some of the best things in life are experiences. Traveling to new and exotic (or the same and routine) locations, trying novel food, meeting different people, listening to innovative music all add to our lives. College is at or near the top of great life experiences.

Colleges are full of interesting, smart, vibrant young adults. It is a great place to meet people with similar *and* different interests. You have the option of attending events, joining clubs, trading ideas about music, movies and sports.

COLLEGE PREPARES YOU FOR CHANGE. Meeting new people, doing different things, exposing yourself to new activities helps you learn how to deal with change. In today's rapidly fluctuating world, it is not only what you know but also how quickly you adapt to varying circumstances. College teaches you how to learn.

COLLEGE IS A PLACE WHERE YOU ARE EXPECTED TO HAVE FUN. It is expected that on warm fall days you stay outside and play Frisbee. It is expected that for a week in the spring you travel to a beach in Florida or Mexico or a mountain in Colorado or South America.

COLLEGE IS A GREAT TIME TO GROW AS AN INDIVIDUAL, to learn, to experience, to become an adult, and to grow into yourself as a person. There are few occasions where you get the opportunity to find out so much about yourself.

Reasons to Stay In College

IF A STUDENT IS LOOKING FOR AN EXCUSE TO DROP OUT OF COLLEGE, THEY WILL ALWAYS FIND ONE. It is too expensive. I'll never get the job I want anyway. I miss my family. It is too far away from my friends. I need to be closer to my girlfriend. The professors are out to get me. The administration is not helping me. The list of excuses is endless.

The first year, sometimes year and a half, is typically the hardest part of college. It is a new situation, there are unfamiliar surroundings and it can be overwhelming. **KEEP IN MIND THAT THE FIRST YEAR OR SO IS THE HARDEST WITH EVERYTHING.** The first year at a new job, living in a new city is the most difficult. For practically everything new, there is often an initial euphoria for a few days, weeks or month. Then the novelty wears off, and we struggle a little (or a lot) with the change until we adapt.

Sometimes we get so focused on the negatives that we forget about the positive aspects of something. This certainly can happen in college. In the middle of a semester it is easy to get bogged down in the mundane aspects of reading textbooks and studying for tests. Some students lose track of the big picture.

The ability to persevere through changes and difficult situations is tough for most of us. **GETTING THROUGH COLLEGE ONE SEMESTER AT A TIME SHOWS PERSEVERANCE.** You get a sense of accomplishment by making it through each semester. You achieved something. It is concrete; the registrar's office has a record showing that you have completed a certain number of credit hours towards graduation. **These accomplishments build confidence.** If you learn how to persevere in college, you will be better able to persist in other areas later in life.

College gives you the opportunity to work on life skills and people skills. There are different types of intelligence: book smart, street smart, common sense, emotional intelligence. College gives you the opportunity to work on all of these. College also helps you work on stress management; it helps develop intellectual curiosity and otherwise provides venues to improve yourself. It also **helps develop or improve work habits.**

We all want to belong, feel important, or be part of something; **at college you have the opportunity to be somebody special.** You can be a radio disc jockey, the captain of the debate team, the president of the finance club, or a leader of innumerable other organizations. You can explore things you didn't even know existed before. You will develop your identity and discover your uniqueness.

> **Keep in mind that the first year or so is the hardest. Getting through college one semester at a time shows perseverance.**
>
> **Perseverance leads to accomplishments, which lead to increased self-confidence.**

Reasons to Finish College

Finishing college leads to better jobs and careers. People with a college degree on average earn much more over their lifetime than people who only finish high school. Money is one reason to stay. Certainly some people don't need to finish college in order to make a lot of money. Many people know that Bill Gates dropped out of Harvard before finishing his degree and it certainly has not hurt his pocketbook. What people don't know is that Steve Ballmer was a friend of Gates' at school. He finished his degree, later got an MBA at Stanford and later became CEO of Microsoft (and is now owner of the Los Angeles Clippers). College helped Ballmer learn and develop skills that he has used over his life.

Once you finish, **a college degree is something no one can ever take from you.** It is an accomplishment, a statement of identity.

I think **the best reason to finish college is the doors that it opens. A college degree gives you alternatives.** You may want to spend your life working at something that does not require a college degree, which is great. But it is better to choose that profession and have alternatives than not to.

I have two friends who are very similar in many aspects. They are both easy going, a little goofy and pretty smart. One, through some ups and downs and struggles got a college degree; the other dropped out of college after a year. While in their twenty's both of them moved from job to job. The one who finished college worked for the Federal Reserve, at another government agency, a large pharmaceutical company and is now at a nonprofit organization. The one without a college degree worked as a short order cook, as a clerk in a liquor store and is now a school bus driver. All of these are admirable and if that is what you choose to do, that is great.

The bus driver is trying to find another job. He has been having difficulty with his search because he doesn't have many options. He's unhappy because he feels trapped. My other friend may or may not move from his job with the non-profit organization. He is happy with his current position, but knows that if he wants he can move back to corporate America or government or somewhere else. It is his choice; he has more options based in part on his college degree.

It is great to work as a bus driver or to put in a hard day of work at anything. The people who are happiest working as bus drivers or anything else are happy because they chose that job, that that is what they want to do. People who are working at a certain job because they have no other options are often not happy.

You may need a little more training to change jobs or careers. You can do this for social work, teaching, or business. It is easier with a college degree because you just need to get a certificate or a Master's degree, usually 30 or so credit hours.

There are a few things in my life that I just gave up on. I played football and baseball in high school for a little while. Within a few years I quit both sports. I made all sorts of excuses: I'll never play in college or beyond so why do it now? This coach doesn't like me. That coach plays favorites. My other friends quit. My parents don't care. The football coach is just an SOB. **IT WAS EASY TO JUSTIFY QUITTING.**

The truth is I was afraid and I gave up. I was afraid that I might be cut from the team. I was afraid that I wouldn't be good enough. I'll never know for sure but my guess is that if I stuck with it and worked very hard I would have ended up as an average player on mediocre high school teams. But I will never know because I was a quitter.

> FINISHING COLLEGE GIVES YOU A SENSE OF SELF-WORTH, AN INNER STRENGTH THAT YOU CAN ONLY GET FROM YOURSELF OR BY ACCOMPLISHING SOMETHING YOURSELF.

Looking back I can see that the football coach was a good guy. I bet that if I had gone to him for a little guidance he would have given it to me. But I didn't. I didn't know any better. He was probably a lot like I am with my students. I have hundreds of students a year. I see some quitting. Sometimes I make an effort to help, but I have hundreds of others who are trying and are responsive to my efforts. I don't have the time or energy to force a student to do something they don't want to. Why should my high school football coach try to force me to stay when it was clear I didn't want to? Why should I try to force somebody to stay in college?

I will always regret having quit. Not because I would have been some great athlete but because I know I could have done better. I, as with almost everybody else have never regretted finishing something I set out to do. My PhD was a lot of work, writing this book was not easy. I wish I had been a better student as an undergraduate, but I am glad I finished college. It gave me a sense of self-worth, an inner strength that you can only get from yourself by accomplishing something yourself.

It seems that some students want to flunk out. From the first day of class, they show up, put their heads down on the desk, spend the entire class texting, don't pay attention, and don't try to make friends with other people in the class. Typically they fail miserably, which is no surprise. It is apparent that they do not want to be in college. I have seen hundreds of students who are miserable in college. They are only there because their parents or some-body else wants them there. **IT IS UP TO YOU TO WANT TO BE IN COLLEGE, AND YOU HAVE TO DO THINGS TO MAKE YOURSELF WANT TO BE THERE.**

During college you will get guidance and help from your parents, professors, other students and perhaps from advisors, coaches and others. But ultimately the impetus is on you to start, continue and finish college. **YOUR SUCCESS (OR FAILURE) IS IN YOUR HANDS. YOU HAVE TO WANT TO LEARN, YOU HAVE TO WANT TO SUCCEED.**

> IT IS UP TO YOU
> TO WANT TO BE IN
> COLLEGE, AND YOU
> HAVE TO DO THINGS
> TO MAKE YOURSELF
> WANT TO BE THERE.
>
> YOUR SUCCESS
> (OR FAILURE)
> IS IN YOUR HANDS.
>
> YOU HAVE TO WANT
> TO LEARN,
> YOU HAVE TO WANT
> TO SUCCEED!

REMEMBER...

College prepares you for change.

College is a place where you are expected to
have fun!

College is a great time to grow
as an individual.

Getting through college one semester at a
time shows perseverance.

College gives you the opportunity to work on
life skills and people skills.

College helps you develop or improve
work habits.

In college, you have the opportunity to
be somebody special.

A college degree is something no one
can ever take from you.

The best reason to finish college is the doors
that it opens. A college degree gives you
alternatives.

Your success is in your hands. You have to
want to learn, you have to want to succeed!

ABOUT THE AUTHOR

Dr. ANSTINE is a professor of management at North Central College. Over the past two and a half decades he has taught dozens of different classes at five colleges and universities. He completed his undergraduate work at the State University of New York at Albany (SUNYA), then worked in New York City for a few years before getting his Doctorate from the University of Kentucky.

49215291R00060

Made in the USA
San Bernardino, CA
17 May 2017